All About Child Care and Early Education

Custom Edition

by Marilyn Segal, Betty Bardige, Mary Jean Woika and Jesse Leinfelder

Taken from:

All About Child Care and Early Education: A Comprehensive Resource for Child Care Professionals
by Marilyn Segal, Betty Bardige, Mary Jean Woika and Jesse Leinfelder

Taken from:

All About Child Care and Early Education: A Comprehensive Resource for Child Care Professionals
by Marilyn Segal, Betty Bardige, Mary Jean Woika and Jesse Leinfelder
Copyright © 2006 by Pearson Education
Published by Allyn and Bacon
Boston, Massachusetts 02116

This special edition is published in cooperation with Pearson Custom Publishing.

All trademarks, service marks, registered trademarks, and registered service marks are the property of their respective owners and are used herein for identification purposes only.

Printed in the United States of America

10 9 8 7 6 5 4 3 2 1

ISBN 0-536-17423-7

2005220211

EH

Please visit our web site at *www.pearsoncustom.com*

PEARSON CUSTOM PUBLISHING
75 Arlington Street, Suite 300, Boston, MA 02116
A Pearson Education Company

Contents

Section I

Setting the Stage

Ensuring a Safe, Healthy, and Appropriate Learning Environment

Miss Disgruntled was talking with her colleague, Ms. Cool-Headed.

Miss Disgruntled: *"What a day! I feel like going home tonight and never coming back."*

Ms. Cool-Headed: *"You sound pretty upset. What's the matter?"*

Miss Disgruntled: *"What's the matter? Everything is the matter. Ever since we got our new director, she's given me nothing but trouble. Yesterday, she came into my room with this whole long list of complaints. My cribs were too close together, and I was endangering the health of the babies. My diapering supplies weren't close enough to the changing table. I had too much stuff on my shelves, and I couldn't possibly keep them all sterile. A couple of boxes were in front of the doors, and if there happened to be a fire, I couldn't get the kids out fast enough."*

Ms. Cool-Headed: *"I know what you mean. Ms. Striver is a real stickler when it comes to health and safety. Did you fix up the room?"*

Miss Disgruntled: *"I worked so hard. I stayed here until 8 o'clock last night rearranging the cribs, taking the toys off the shelves, throwing out the trash, and clearing off the shelf by the diaper area to make room for the diaper supplies."*

Ms. Cool-Headed: *"Ms. Striver must have been happy when she saw your room in the morning."*

Miss Disgruntled: *"Happy? Not one word of thanks or 'You did a good job.' All she said was that now if I wanted my room to be a safe and healthy place for children, I'd better make it more attractive. Now what does making a room attractive have to do with health and safety?"*

Ms. Cool-Headed knew perfectly well what the director was trying to tell Miss Disgruntled, but she also knew that this was not the time to talk about it. Instead, she said, "Go home and get a good rest, and I'll help you with the room tomorrow."

Both Ms. Cool-Headed and Ms. Striver recognize that a room that is uninviting might very well be a safety hazard for young children. All young children need to be in an environment that is attractive and homelike. They need large spaces for active play and smaller, more intimate places for quiet play. In a well-designed classroom, the noise level is controlled and age-appropriate toys are in reach and displayed in an organized fashion. There are places where children can gather in small groups and places where children can be alone or with one other friend. A well-designed classroom is a safe and healthy place where children can play and learn.

Safety

Chapter 1

Overview

Safety involves preventing the injury of children and adults.

Rationale

Following the old adage "Safety first" is especially important for those who are responsible for young children. Young children depend on adults to keep them safe; they do not yet have the knowledge, skills, or judgment to keep themselves out of danger. Therefore, it is the teacher's responsibility to create and maintain a safe environment while also helping children to learn safety skills.

Although as jobs go, caring for young children is relatively safe, teachers do need to be conscious of their own safety as well as the children's. Even a minor accident, resulting in a wrenched back or twisted ankle, can prevent a teacher from doing her job.

Objectives

1. To learn how to plan safe activities by taking into account children's developmental levels and likely behaviors

2. To learn how to create and maintain safe classroom and playground environments

3. To review what to do in case of a medical emergency

4. To learn safe practices for taking children on field trips

5. To develop and model good safety habits

6. To learn how to involve preschool children in developing safety rules for their classroom

7. To learn how to develop a safety curriculum

8. To learn how to set up a safe environment for children with special needs

Providing a Safe Learning Environment

Miss Carefree felt good about the safety record of her classroom. "Since the beginning of the year," she boasted, "not one child in my class has gotten hurt. Keeping children safe is no big deal," she went on. "All you have to do is keep a good eye on the kids."

While good supervision is certainly the most important safety rule, if we are really committed to keeping children safe, we cannot rely on supervision alone. In this chapter, we describe how teachers demonstrate their commitment to safety.

To learn how to plan safe activities by taking into account children's developmental levels and likely behaviors

Miss Full-of-Energy had been chided by the director, who told her that her classroom was out of control. "My classroom was not out of control," Miss Full-of-Energy insisted. "When you came into the room, they were playing Follow-the-Leader. It was just too bad that Kimberly bumped her head when she tried to jump off the chair, but she really didn't get hurt."

Miss Full-of-Energy should be commended for wanting her class to have fun. At the same time, she should realize that a rowdy, chair-climbing game of Follow-the-Leader is not appropriate for 2-year-olds. Two-year-olds are great imitators. When one child performs a feat like jumping off a chair, the other children will want to do the same thing, even if they don't have the skills to do it safely.

The first rule of safety is *prevention.* A safety-minded teacher must be aware of age-related norms and characteristics (see the Developmental Picture feature). She must also be aware of the characteristic behaviors of individual children. Kimberly was a daring child, although not physically adept. When another child performed a physical feat, Kimberly was bound to follow suit. Her fall from the chair was an accident waiting to happen.

> *The first rule of safety is prevention.*

Developmental Picture

The young infant (0–9 months):

- Is developing new skills day by day, such as rolling over, reaching, putting things in her mouth, pulling on things, and scooting

The caregiver:
- Childproofs the areas used by infants
- Never leaves infants unattended
- Provides a clean, protected floor space where infants can lay down, push up, roll over, and crawl
- Provides safe toys infants can touch and mouth

The older infant (9–14 months):

- Is learning new motor skills at a very fast rate, such as scooting, creeping, pulling up, climbing, and toddling from place to place

The caregiver:
- Cleans and childproofs the areas and supervises closely
- Provides safe, low, and sturdy structures for babies to pull up on and climb on
- Provides appropriate outdoor surfaces for crawling and toddling, such as blankets, clean sand, and outdoor carpeting

The young toddler (14–24 months):

- Is likely to develop a special interest in opening and shutting doors and drawers, picking up and mouthing small toys and objects, standing on top of things, and crawling into spaces that are hard to get out of

The caregiver:
- Safetyproofs indoor and outdoor areas, making sure there are no dangers that children can get into (thumb tacks, glass, sharp table edges, shelf units that can topple, loose rugs, etc.)

The older toddler (2 years):

- Is developing new motor skills, such as walking and going down stairs
- Is apt to run or dart from place to place but is not good at stopping
- Is curious and unable to identify dangers
- Is likely to imitate the feats of older children even when they are beyond his ability
- May be impulsive and dash into new places
- Investigates and experiments with throwing hard objects or hitting with sticks

(continued)

The caregiver:

- Makes sure that there are no places in the classroom or on the playground where a child cannot be seen or can escape from
- Makes sure that the 2-year-old has no opportunity to explore or play with dangerous things like matches, pills, poisonous plants, and cleaning fluids
- Recognizes that electric fans, balloons, and plastic bags are potentially dangerous

The preschooler (3–5 years):

- Is frequently a risk taker, especially with large-muscle activities
- Is gaining the ability to consider safety and is ready to learn safety rules
- Learns safe practices through experiences
- Is insistent about doing things for herself and does not like to hold hands while crossing a road, put on a safety belt, or let an adult help when she is climbing down or jumping

The caregiver:

- Provides a safe environment with careful supervision
- Teaches safe practices and safety concepts

Think about the young children you know, or skip ahead to the developmental overviews at the beginning of Section II (pages 19–26). Based on your observations or these descriptions, think about the following:

- Which of the activities listed below would be safe for preschoolers but not for younger children?
- Which would be safe for toddlers but not for infants?
- Which would be safe for children of all ages?
- Which would not be safe for children under 6?
- What conditions or child characteristics would make these activities safe or unsafe?

Activities

- Blowing and watching soap bubbles
- Dodge ball
- Tricycle races
- A game of chase or tag involving 10 children
- Drawing with chalk on a sidewalk
- A game of musical chairs
- Finger painting with shaving cream

Objective 2

To learn how to create and maintain safe classroom and playground environments

Mrs. Happy-Go-Lucky was in great spirits. She had just made a tour of the infant/toddler room, and it looked beautiful. There were pictures tacked up on all the walls at eye level for the children. There were hanging plants with textured leaves that even babies could touch. There was a floor fan in the infant area that made the mobiles spin. There were jars of marbles on the table near the window that reflected the rays of the sun. There were pillows in the shapes of turtles in all of the infant cribs. ●

As you can imagine, Mrs. Happy-Go-Lucky was not so happy after her supervisor inspected the classroom. Can you find five potential hazards that need to be removed?

A good beginning for thinking about the safety of a classroom or a playground is to identify the kinds of accidents that are likely to occur. In a classroom, children can get hurt by falling down, by having something fall on them, by bumping into something sharp, by getting an electric shock, by ingesting something harmful, by getting fingers pinched in doors or drawers, by getting cut with something sharp, by getting burned, or by being hit or poked by another child. Infants can suffocate on a surface that is too soft, if they roll onto their stomachs and then can't turn their faces to get a breath. (That is why parents and caregivers are taught to put infants to sleep on their backs and to provide firm surfaces for infants to lie on when they are awake.) On the playground, children can get hurt by falling off something high, by falling on something sharp or hard, by colliding with something, by getting hit by something, by getting a part of their body caught or pinched, by eating or touching a poisonous plant, or by getting a splinter.

No matter how careful we are, we cannot prevent all accidents. But by looking at the kinds of accidents that can happen, we can recognize ways to reduce the risks.

Safety in the Classroom

Once you have thought about the kinds of accidents that can happen, take a close look at the classroom you work in and see if you can answer the following questions:

- Are all potentially dangerous materials safely out of reach of children, even children who can climb? (This includes cleaning materials, medicines, poisonous plants, sharp scissors or knives, electric cords, hot drinks, and so on.)
- Are all electrical outlets covered?
- Are there no sharp edges on tables or ledges that children could run into?
- Is the floor clear of obstacles, loose rugs, and wet spots that could cause a child to trip or slip?
- Have any dangling cords been removed or secured, so that a child cannot get tangled in them or pull on them and cause something to fall?
- Are heavy pieces of furniture—including bookshelves, highchairs, and folding tables—secure and stable, so that they cannot be tipped over by children who climb, push, pull, or swing?
- Do you know where the fire extinguisher is and how to use it, and are you sure it works?
- Are all the toys in good repair and safe for the developmental ages of the children in the group?

- Have objects that can be swallowed or have small parts been removed, if there are children under 3?
- Are the room dividers low enough so that you can see all the children at any one time?
- Are there appropriate precautions and adaptations for children with allergies, physical limitations, and other special health needs?

Safety on the Playground

Now it is time to go out to the playground and ask a second set of questions:

- Is the playground area securely fenced off, with safety locks on all gates?
- Is the playground clear of broken glass and other debris?
- Are there railings and walk spaces on the tops of slides to prevent falls?
- Are the S-hooks tightly closed on all the swings? Are all the chains and ropes holding the swings in good condition?
- Is the framework of the swings securely mounted by being set in cement?
- Are the swings made of soft, lightweight material, so that a child who walks into an empty moving swing will not be hurt?
- Is there a minimum of 6 (and preferably 8) inches of sand, mulch, or grass under all climbing structures and swing sets?
- Is all equipment free of splinters, cracks, rusted areas, and loose screws and bolts?

- Is metal equipment in the shade, so that children cannot get burned?
- Is the playground surface smooth, with no holes or protruding objects?
- Are the riding paths wide, gently curved, and marked for one-way traffic?
- Has all broken equipment been removed?
- Has the playground been checked for poisonous plants?
- Is all play equipment anchored well in the ground and placed in an area with a safety gate around it? (Barriers to younger, inexperienced children should be placed around dangerous climbing structures, reserving them for only those children who are capable of getting around the barriers. Swings should be placed in an easily supervised area that is isolated from other playground traffic.)
- Are there appropriate precautions and adaptations for children with allergies, physical limitations, and other special health needs?

Complying with Safety Standards

Mrs. Cautious was visiting different child care centers. She wanted to find a center where she could be sure her son would be safe. When she entered the classroom where her child would be placed, she heard the director talking to the teacher. "Please move those boxes, Miss Rule-Bender. They are blocking the exit." Miss Rule-Bender immediately apologized. "I'll move them right after class," she promised. "I completely forgot that the fire department is coming tomorrow morning." Mrs. Cautious decided she would find a different place for her son.

Every state establishes minimum safety standards for licensing child care establishments. Although the stringency of these standards differs among states, all states require that child care establishments adhere to fire safety standards and are monitored by the fire department on a regular basis. The purpose of standards is to protect children from harm. No one expects that there will be a fire in a child care center, and the chances of it happening are certainly slim. Unfortunately, even slim chances do happen, and when we are responsible for children's safety, even the slimmest chance is too great a risk.

Every family child care home and child care center needs to have an evacuation plan in case of a fire or other emergency. This plan should include routes out of the building, what to bring along, and what to do before leaving. The plan should be posted in a public place and practiced through regular fire drills.

To review what to do in case of a medical emergency

If you are working with young children, you should have up-to-date training and certification in first aid and cardiopulmonary resuscitation (CPR). Since recommendations change frequently in response to new research, it is important to keep your certification current.

Your center or family child care home should have policies in place so that everyone can respond promptly in case of a medical emergency—for instance:

- Emergency supplies should be stored in a place that is accessible to adults but not to children.
- Contact information for all families, as well as information on children's known allergies and other special medical needs, should be kept in a secure and readily accessible place.
- *In an emergency, first call 911.* Then call the child's parents or emergency contact. When you call 911, be sure to state the problem briefly and clearly, including the age of the child. Give your program's full address and telephone number. (This information should be posted on or near each telephone.)

First Aid Guidelines

Locate and become familiar with sources of up-to-date information about first aid practices. On the website of the Mayo Clinic are guidelines that reflect the recommendations of specialists, adapted from their Medi-Smart First Aid Guidelines (2004). To access these guidelines, go to www.medi-smart.com/fa-mayo.htm.

Objective 4

To learn safe practices for taking children on field trips

Field trips can be great fun or absolutely disastrous. The outcome depends less on chance than on careful planning. The most important thing to plan for is the safety of the children. Use these points as a checklist to help take the risks out of field trips:

- Visit the field trip site in person ahead of time.
- Get a signed permission slip for each child.
- Recruit parents to help you on the field trip.
- Prepare the children for the field trip by reviewing where they are going, how they will get there, and what safety rules they will need to follow. Be sure to teach them the name of their center or program, in case they get separated from the group.
- Dress the children in matching tee-shirts, preferably ones imprinted with the center's or program's name and address.
- If you are going by car, make sure that there is a seatbelt for every person in the car and a car seat for each child under 3 (or whatever your state requires).
- Bring along the permission slips, a first aid kit, and the emergency phone numbers of all the children.
- Make sure that each child is paired with a buddy.
- Use the travel time to sing songs and tell stories.
- Count the children at least once every 15 minutes and before moving to a new area.

Objective 5

To develop and model good safety habits

After a good two hours of extra work, Mrs. Happy-Go-Lucky completed the job of childproofing her classroom. She was standing on a little chair, putting away the marbles, when her supervisor returned to the room. "Get down from that chair this minute!" her supervisor insisted. "That's a good way to break a leg!" Poor Mrs. Happy-Go-Lucky! She wasn't allowed to leave the center until she had studied the safe practices list. ●

Keeping Yourself Safe

Maintaining safe patterns of behavior includes much more than keeping your classroom and playground free of hazards. It also involves keeping yourself safe.

Here is an adult safety checklist that one center compiled after keeping track of the kinds of accidents that had occurred there over the past several years:

- Bend your knees and use your legs, rather than your back, to lift heavy objects and children.
- Don't carry more than one child at a time.
- Use a stepladder for reaching high shelves.
- Dry the floor after washing it or after mopping up a wet spill.
- When using a sharp knife or tool, make sure that you will not be bumped or distracted by active children. If children are nearby, ask them to sit down and watch you or give them jobs of their own.
- Do not use or demonstrate child-sized furniture or equipment that is not designed to support an adult.
- Use common sense, and don't take risks.
- Do not hesitate to ask another adult for help.

Keeping Children Safe

Young children are notoriously unpredictable. Safety-conscious teachers know that they cannot eliminate every danger or intercept every fall. But they can practice some basic safety habits and teach children to behave safely. Teachers can demonstrate their commitment to safety by doing the following:

- Supervise the children at all times.
- Count the children whenever you move to a new area to be sure that none are left behind.
- Keep the door to your classroom closed but not latched. (You can put a bell or chime on the door to alert you when someone is leaving or entering.)
- Model safe behavior.
- Show children the safe way to climb up or down, sit on a swing, carry something heavy or awkward, knock down a block tower, handle a tool, or use playground equipment.
- Don't give children foods that may cause choking, including popcorn, whole grapes, ice cubes, nuts, seeds, raw carrot rounds, hard candy, and corn chips.
- Plan and practice fire drills.
- Release children only to those who are authorized to pick them up; check the IDs of unfamiliar parents.

Helping Parents Follow Good Safety Practices

Many of the accidents and emergencies that occur at preschools involve parents and occur during busy drop-off and pick-up times. For instance, a child may run into the traffic lane while his parent is talking to a friend or strapping a younger sibling into a car seat. A rushed parent may accidentally lock a child in a car or give in to his pleas to sit in the front seat or stay out of the car seat. A child may wander into an unsupervised area while her parent is gathering her belongings.

To avoid these mishaps, you may want to make a safety discussion part of an early parent meeting, send home a safety flyer, or post reminder notices on the parent bulletin board or in other appropriate spots. Here are some points to cover:

- Young children should always ride in the back seat of a car in a safety-approved car seat that has been installed correctly. (You might invite a parent volunteer or police officer to do a safety check, if parents have questions.)
- Children should be carried or held by the hand when entering or leaving the center.
- Everyone should take care to close the door slowly and firmly upon entering or leaving the center.
- Children can only be released to authorized persons.
- Drivers should follow a clearly marked, one-way traffic pattern, if possible.
- Extra caution should be used when backing out of parking spaces.
- Parents are responsible for supervising their children if they use the playground when the center is not officially open.

If parents and staff feel it is necessary, you can station a staff person or parent volunteer outside during drop-off and pick-up times.

In addition, you will want to share general child safety information with parents. Parents of infants should be reminded of the "Back to Sleep" campaign to reduce sudden infant death syndrome (SIDS) by having babies sleep on their backs. All parents should be given information about local safety and first aid courses and product recalls. They should be reminded of the dangers of second-hand smoke and of having guns in the home. Parents should have opportunities to bring up any concerns that they may have, as well.

Finally, you will want to help parents talk with their children about safety issues, especially if there has been an accident or a scare in your neighborhood. Brainstorm ways of reassuring the children and of teaching commonsense precautions without inducing fear.

To learn how to involve preschool children in developing safety rules for their classroom

Mr. Nose-to-the-Grindstone dropped into his daughter's prekindergarten classroom during morning circle time. The children were helping the teacher draw up a list of safety rules for the classroom. The red-headed boy suggested "No hitting or kicking." The class agreed that that was a good rule, and it was added to the list. Next, the girl with the ponytail shouted out that she knew one: "Nobody should drop their juice pop on the floor." The boy beside her chimed in, "That's a dumb rule. I don't ever eat juice pops. They are yucky." The teacher asked the group if it was all right to drop any kind of food on the floor. One child said, "Maybe you can't help it if you drop something on the floor. Like it could be an accident." The girl with the ponytail agreed. "Maybe we should say if you drop food or something on the floor, you should clean it up." "And you shouldn't throw blocks at people," the boy in the red shirt added. "Good thinking," the teacher commented, as she wrote down the two new rules.

Mr. Nose-to-the-Grindstone left the room and went right to the director. "You've got to have a talk with that teacher," he told the director. "Instead of teaching these kids something, she has them sitting in a circle making up safety rules." ●

Despite Mr. Nose-to-the-Grindstone's assertion, the teacher was teaching the class something. First, she was helping the children think about behaviors that could cause someone to get hurt. Second, she was teaching them that creating a safety rule is a way of preventing an accident. Third and most important, the teacher recognized that older preschool children are likely to follow rules that they have helped to create.

> *Children are likely to follow rules that they have helped to create.*

As you read the following lists of rules that were developed by a class of 4-year-olds, think about which of them would be appropriate for your classroom and what other rules you would add.

Safety Rules for the Classroom
(In the words of 4-year-olds)

- No running.
- Sit on chairs but don't stand on chairs or on tables either.
- You shouldn't point things at people, like scissors.
- You don't leave the classroom unless your teacher says it's okay.
- You don't fool around with electric outlets or things like that.

Safety Rules for the Playground
(Also in the words of 4-year-olds)

- You have to sit in the middle of the swing and you can't stand up and you stop it before you get off.
- One at a time on the slide and you have to go down frontwards.
- You don't bump into people when you ride your tricycles.
- You don't say "Ha-ha, Scaredy-cat" if somebody is scared to go on the jungle gym.

Objective 7
To learn how to develop a safety curriculum

In addition to childproofing the classroom, modeling safe behavior, and developing safety rules, teachers can help children become safety conscious by including safety lessons in their lesson plans. Here are some ideas for activities.

Activities for Improving Safety

Go on a Safety Walk

Objective: To teach children to recognize and talk about potential hazards

Procedure: Give each child a red circle sticker. Ask the children to walk around the classroom (or the playground) and put their red stickers on things that could be dangerous. In circle time, ask children where they put their stickers and what the dangers are.

Play a Freeze! Game

Objective: To teach children to respond immediately to the word *stop*

Procedure: Make two parallel lines on the playground using crepe paper or yarn. Line the children up on the starting line. When you say "Go," ask the children to begin walking toward the finish line. When you say "Stop," all the children must stop on the spot. If the children keep moving when you say "Stop," they must go back to start. Add an element of cooperation by having the children walk in pairs.

Read a Story

Objective: To teach children about safety

Procedure: Read children a safety story in circle time. Allow them to talk about experiences in which they have had to practice good safety.

"Fire Station" Pretend Play

Objective: To teach children to dial 911 in case of a fire

Procedure: Turn your pretend play area into a fire station and encourage the children to play "fire station." For props, use a telephone, fire hats (which you could make as a craft), a bell, a length of hose, whistles, and some blankets. Help the children play out a scenario in which someone sees smoke and dials 911. The call is received in the "fire station." Someone rings the bell, and the children get out the hose, rush to the fire, and put it out.

Safety Walk

Objective: To teach traffic safety

Procedure: Take the children for a safety walk on the playground. Pretend the path is a busy street. (If you do not have a path on your playground, make a path out of rope or mark one with chalk.) Use a yardstick with red on one end and green on the other as a signal. Teach the children to walk to the end of the road, wait until the light turns green, look both ways, and say "All clear" before they cross.

Safety Crafts

Objective: To reinforce awareness of safety

Procedure: Children can make all sorts of pretend play props: fire hats, safety badges, 911 signs to put by the phone, and even a working traffic light (with green, red, and yellow paper covering holes cut in a milk carton that they can shine a flashlight through). As children incorporate these crafts in their play, you can talk together about safe practices.

Field Trip

Objective: To increase safety consciousness

Procedure: Take a trip to a fire station or police station, or invite a police officer or fire marshal to come to your center. Encourage the children to ask questions. After the trip or visit, help children work together to make a list of things they learned or to draw pictures for a class book about safety.

To learn how to set up a safe environment for children with special needs

Prior to the opening day, the director of Open Arms Nursery School was telling the staff about the new children who were enrolled in their classes. "There are three children in your class who were not in the school last year," she told Mrs. Keep Safe. "There's Jim, who is Cornelia's younger brother; Jacques, whose family recently immigrated from Haiti; and Madeline, who is quite a self-sufficient child, although she is legally blind."

Mrs. Keep Safe turned pale. "I would be happy to have Jim and Jacques, but I must admit I am worried about having a blind child in my class. You know the children in my class are quite active, and I feel a blind child might get hurt. As far as I am concerned, my first obligation is to keep the children safe."

"You worry too much," the director responded. "I used to teach in a school where almost half of the children in the class had some sort of disability, and we had a perfect safety record. As a matter of fact, I just read an article about how children with disabilities in an inclusive school are less likely to get hurt than typically developing children. The article went on to say that typically developing preschool children are protective of children with special needs and are careful not to hurt them."

"Well, okay," Mrs. Keep Safe agreed. "I guess I'll give it a try." ●

The director of Open Arms Nursery School is absolutely right. Children with special needs are less likely to get hurt in a preschool setting than are typically developing children. Nevertheless, teachers and caregivers of children with special needs must remain continually vigilant and anticipate the kinds of accidents related to children's disabilities that could occur and take preventive measures.

Setting Up a Safe Indoor Environment

The kinds of modifications needed to make the classroom safe for a child with a disability depends very much on the nature of the disability. Many children with conditions such as mild retardation and language delays do not require any special room arrangements. Children with physical or sensory limitations, however, may benefit from some adaptations. Modifications needed in the classroom may include raising or lowering a table, making a bathroom wheelchair accessible, and being extra careful to ensure that there are no sharp corners on tables or shelves and that doorways are barrier free.

> *Children with special needs are less likely to get hurt in a preschool setting than are typically developing children.*

In addition to the room arrangement, children with special needs may need special equipment and materials. Children who are visually impaired may need a braille computer, large-print books, or a magnifying glass. Children who are hearing impaired may need a hearing aid or language board. Children who are physically challenged may need a wheelchair, standing table, or chair with special supports. Children with learning problems may need materials such as puzzles or pegboards that are likely to be used with younger children.

Setting Up a Safe Outdoor Environment

Like all children, children with special needs benefit from active play. Again, some modifications will be needed. The kinds of modifications that you make on the playground will depend on the nature of the child's disablity and the recommendation of the parent or therapist. Children who are physically challenged may need to have a balance beam set in the ground, so that they can practice balance without getting hurt, or a tricycle with foot holders that make it easier to pedal.

With a visually impaired child, you may also need to cordon off the area behind the swings or to provide soft Nerf balls for playing circle games. Children who are hearing impaired do not need special equipment, but you may want to use hand signals to give them directions.

Additional Resources about Safety

Caring for Our Children—National health and safety performance standards: Guidelines for out of home child care programs (2nd ed). (2002). Washington, DC: NAEYC. (Updated standards issued jointly by the American Academy of Pediatrics, American Public Health Association, and the National Resource Center for Health and Safety in Child Care)

Section II

On Stage
Supporting Physical and Intellectual Development

Mrs. Try-My-Best, a family child care provider, had the following discussion while having dinner at a restaurant with a friend:

Mrs. Try-My-Best: "Sorry about being late. I was talking to one of my parents about her baby, and she wouldn't let me go."

Friend: "Was she complaining about something?"

Mrs. Try-My-Best: "No, she is a very helpful parent, and she almost never complains. But she wanted me to tell her about her baby, and no matter what I told her, she kept asking me the same question."

Friend: "What was the question?"

Mrs. Try-My-Best: " 'How is my baby developing?' It was strange. I told her how well he was sitting by himself and how he had just learned to pass a toy from one hand to the other. But whatever I told her, she would say, 'That's great, but it's not what I'm asking. I just want you to tell me about my son's development.' "

Although Mrs. Try-My-Best could not figure out what this parent wanted to know, this parent's question is quite legitimate. Knowing how well a child is doing in several domains of development does not answer the question of how well that child is developing overall. Domains of development are interdependent. In order to master a task like picking up a spoon on demand, the child must have the language ability to understand what he is expected to do, the cognitive ability to recognize which object is a spoon, the physical ability to pick up the spoon, and the psychological motivation to do it. A child's *developmental level* refers to the total range of his capacities and resources at a particular point in time.

In this text, we describe several domains of development: physical, cognitive, language, imaginative or creative, emotional, and social. Each of these domains is described in its own chapter. The emotional and social domains are touched on in the first part of this section but described in more detail in the next.

This approach allows us to focus on the expected developmental sequences in each domain and to suggest activities to reinforce existing skills and to encourage the development of emerging skills at each stage. The downside of this approach is that it does not provide a wide-angled picture of the expected developmental status of children at different ages. In the developmental overviews that follow, we present a global picture of child development at age points from birth to 5 years.

Developmental Benchmarks

Benchmark age periods for children from birth to age 3 need to be considered through at least two lenses. Practitioners have become used to thinking of children in one-year increments: 0 to 12 months, 12 to 24 months, and 24 to 36 months. Moreover, child care licensing regulations in many states define specific adult/child ratios and group-size limits according to one-year increments. That practice has contributed to organizing the classrooms in many child care programs along lines of annual chronological age.

In contrast, some child development experts describe development during the months from birth to age 3 according to developmental benchmarks, rather than annual divisions. The following age groupings have been defined by Zero to Three and the CDA Council. (Contact information for these organizations is provided at the end of this section; see page 26.) Note that the descriptive terms used differ slightly, even though they describe the same general characteristics:

Age in Months	Zero to Three	CDA Council
0–8	The early months	Young infants
9–17 or 8–18	Crawlers and walkers	Mobile infants
18–36	Toddlers and 2-year-olds	Toddlers

This text generally uses these benchmark divisions. In the narrative sections and in the Developmental Picture features in each chapter, the following age indicators are used:

0–9 months	Young infants
9–14 months	Older infants
14–24 months	Young toddlers
24–36 months	Older toddlers/2-year-olds

Developmental Overviews
Infants

Following an infant's development is an exciting experience. Infants change from week to week, from day to day, and sometimes from minute to minute. Like busy scientists, they are continually seeking new information, performing experiments, and testing new ideas. Over time, infants discover new things about themselves, as well. They discover ways to kick with their legs, grasp with their hands, and make interesting sounds with their mouths. They discover that people are useful, that language is important, and that an object that is hidden from sight continues to exist. In fact, many behavioral scientists feel that the foundations for all later development—physical, psychological, intellectual, and social—are established within the first year of life. This means that the kinds of experiences we provide for babies are extremely important and can have a lifelong impact.

Before zeroing in on the kind of curriculum that would be appropriate for babies, let us look at the characteristics of babies at different ages so we know what to expect.

Young Infants

Birth to Three Months

Although we may think of a newborn baby as being fragile and helpless, he comes into this world with an impressive set of built-in reflexes and adaptive behaviors. He looks into his mother's eyes and attends to the sound of her voice. He closes his eyes in response to bright lights and reflexively grasps a finger when it is placed in his palm. Within the first three months, a baby will make connections among feelings, sights, and sounds. When he hears the sound of a rattle, he will search for it with his eyes. Upon seeing a smiling face, he will respond with a smile and a coo.

At first, babies respond more to what is happening *inside* them than to what is happening *outside* them. Then there is a gradual turning outward—an awakening to the world outside. A baby who is held, rocked, sung to, smiled at, and loved begins to make some early connections between the sound of a special person's voice and the smile on that person's face or the sensation of being rocked. A baby who is played with, cuddled, and soothed learns to associate the presence of a caregiver with a sense of well-being.

As caregivers, our goals and activities during these early months are designed to help the infant develop her emerging capacities. We help her to focus her eyes and follow moving targets. We encourage the baby to listen and respond to different sounds. We provide special exercises to help her relax and gain muscle tone. Alert caregivers recognize the infant's needs. There are times when infants need stimulation and times when soothing them is more appropriate. We must try to recognize and respond to each baby's rhythm and to adjust our activities and routines to her individual needs.

Three to Six Months

From 3 to 6 months old, infants are learning to explore the world with their hands as well as with their eyes. Learning to reach out is dependent on having something to reach for. If an interesting gym is strung across a baby's crib, she will bat at it, watch it move in response to the batting, and bat at it again. This tendency to repeat an action that creates an interesting effect shows the infant's first intuitive recognition of her own ability to affect her environment.

At about the same time babies are making discoveries about their emerging ability to make things happen, they are also discovering things about their social world. They have learned to smile and coo at a caregiver and to expect a cooing response, and they are developing their first conversational skills. With appropriate experience, a baby will learn to draw the caregiver into an interaction; to coo back and forth, taking turns with her partner; and to imitate simple cooing sounds.

During these next three months, infants become more responsive and less irritable. Their interest in environmental exploration increases. Important developments include social smiling, hand watching, hand play, the gradual development of increasingly precise reaching skills, interest in playing with toys, rolling over, and by the end of the sixth month, progress in learning to sit. This is an important time for face-to-face interaction between the infant and the caregiver.

Activities for caregivers during the 3- to 6-month period are designed to give the baby an opportunity to practice these new and emerging skills. Motor activities enhance balance and muscle strength in preparation for crawling and sitting. Activities with rattles and squeak toys encourage manipulation and hand/eye coordination. Language and cooing games encourage making new sounds and engaging in social interaction.

Six to Nine Months

By the age of 6 to 9 months, the baby has begun to drop things on purpose and then look for them, to bang objects on a hard surface, and to transfer things from hand to hand. He is beginning to have a crude notion of *object permanence* (something continues to exist even when we can't see it) and can imitate simple actions (like banging) that he has already learned. In the next three months, the infant's notions about objects will become more sophisticated, and by the end of the ninth month, he will begin to look for hidden objects.

At this age, the infant will add many more sounds to his vocabulary and will begin babbling ("Mamma," "Dadda," "babba"). He will start to respond to a few specific words, like his name and "Hi," and he may begin to show a wariness of strangers. During this time period, most babies prefer sitting up, and they begin to use some method of crawling. They can drink from a cup with help and will hold his own bottle.

Activities for caregivers during this period are designed to help infants become more sophisticated in their ability to manipulate objects. We provide the infant with a variety of toys that are different in shape, size, and texture and in the sounds they make. How many different things will an infant do with a toy? Does he know that a soft rubber toy is for squeaking and a rattle is for shaking? Do his hands work together when he plays with a toy? As we give infants experience with finger foods, we help to develop their grasping skills. Dropping games are useful as an aid in learning releasing skills. During this period, infants are learning to recognize the patterns and rhythms of language. We introduce songs and nursery rhymes to give infants exposure to the special qualities of language.

Older Infants

Nine to Fourteen Months

From 9 to 14 months is a time when we see many rapid developments. Older infants understand more and more specific words, such as "Mommy," "no," "bottle," and the like. They become interested in looking at books and may start pointing to specific objects. Their babbling starts to sound more like true speech; some babies during this time will start saying words.

Babies' imitative skills also improve, and they begin to imitate new actions. They learn to wave bye-bye and to play Pat-a-Cake. At first, these gestures are imitative—the caregiver waves and then the baby waves. But after a while, the baby responds to the verbal command. Babies at this age may also learn to imitate simple social actions, such as "making nice" to a doll and putting a hat on one's own head.

Older infants' interest in objects shifts from simple manipulation to performing tasks with the objects, like dropping them into a container and throwing or rolling them. Babies learn to use new methods of exploration, such as poking with a finger, and will begin to actively explore objects within reach. Babies perfect the *pincer grasp* (thumb/finger) and enjoy picking up small objects and finger foods.

Older infants are now really on the go. They creep quickly on all fours, pull themselves to a standing position, and cruise sideways along furniture. This new ability to move through space brings with it the potential danger of moving away from Mother or a trusted caregiver. Fortunately, a baby recognizes his caregiver's face, even from a distance, and is able to keep a close watch on that person's whereabouts. For the baby between 9 and 14 months, his mother or caregiver becomes the base of operations. The baby will explore freely as long as his caregiver is in sight.

Caregivers' activities during the 9- to 14-month period are designed to teach understanding of specific words, to encourage the development of object permanence, and to help in learning to imitate simple actions. We also work on developing simple self-help skills and on providing opportunities for infants to explore their rapidly developing motor capacities.

Young Toddlers

Between 14 and 24 months, babies develop at greatly varying rates. Each baby seems to have her own special strengths. Some babies are very social; they like to "talk" and interact a great deal. Others are more interested in their toys. Some babies are concentrating on learning to talk and are not in such a great hurry to run or climb. Others never have the time to stop to talk. They are always on the move—running, climbing, and manipulating.

During this time period, most babies will learn to walk steadily. They will attempt to run, and they will begin to walk up and down stairs. Self-help skills will improve. By 24 months, they should be able to use a cup and spoon fairly well and to help in the dressing process by pulling off their socks, raising their arms, and picking up their feet so their shoes can be put on.

In addition to practicing emerging motor skills, babies between 14 and 24 months have become interested in exploring and experimenting. They are continually searching for objects with moving parts, for things that fit into other things, and for things that can be poured, spilled, carried, or somehow transported. They enjoy toys that can be pushed, pulled, or wheeled around; toys that can be stacked, pounded, or lined up; and toys that respond to their manipulations by making interesting sounds.

At the same time that children show an interest in sound-making toys, they are also likely to expand their own sound-making repertoire. Sometime during the second year, expressive babbling language is converted to meaningful words. Most children by 18 months have a meaningful vocabulary of 15 words. By 2 years old, their vocabulary may include as many as 200 words.

More important, the young toddler is showing quantum leaps in *receptive language*, which is the understanding of spoken words. Babies this age can show you their eyes, nose, mouth, and ears; point to photos of different family members; and follow short, one-word commands. In the course of the second year, there will be a rapid expansion of receptive language and an emerging capacity to listen to a story, watch a video with a story line, and follow a two-step command.

Paralleling the emergence of receptive language is an emerging capacity to imitate behavioral sequences. Young toddlers will jabber on a toy telephone, wipe up a spill, place a key in a lock, smear their faces with makeup, sweep with a broom, and lap up the water from the cat's dish. This imitation of familiar actions is evidence of a child's capacity to think in symbols and is the precursor of pretend play.

Another important development in the second year of life is the emergence of self-awareness. The child is becoming increasingly aware of himself as an actor. If you laugh at something he does, he will promptly do it again to produce another laugh. He is also sensitive to the fact that some of the things that he wants to do are prohibited by adults. When an adult tries to curtail his explorations with a "No," he is likely to persist in what he is doing until he recognizes that he does not have a choice.

The fact that the baby can now choose between conforming and not conforming puts a new strain on the adult. Parents and caregivers are likely to be torn between encouraging exploration and independence and teaching caution, obedience, and responsibility. An overriding concern is that a baby who hears "No" too many times may lose interest in exploring, thus limiting his opportunities to learn.

Older Toddlers (Two-Year-Olds)

The period from 2 to 3 is sometimes known as the "terrible two's." The "No" of the toddler has become a convincing temper tantrum and the 2-year-old is often described as "ornery," "stubborn," and "impossible to live with."

Two-year-olds have, for the most part, earned their reputation. During this period, they are continually exerting authority. The "No's" of the 2-year-old are not simply a way of saying "I don't want it" or "I won't do it." The "No's" are a way of declaring her right to make decisions. Two-year-olds want to do things by themselves, even when that may not be in their best interest.

For the most part, the tantrums of the 2-year-old disappear as long as they are ignored. After all, it is not really worth having a tantrum if no one is going to pay attention. A few children at this age, however, have tantrums as a reaction to being tired, and leaving them alone doesn't change the behavior. For these children, it is usually a good idea to take them out of the situation, hold them quietly but firmly, and invite them back to play when they recover their composure.

Two-year-olds have learned to run and would much rather run than walk, even when they are tired. Although they can run forward at a good pace, most 2-year-olds have not learned how to negotiate a turn or to run around a corner. When 2-year-olds are running on the playground, some bumps and falls are to be expected. Emerging motor skills for 2-year-olds include jumping with their feet together, riding a tricycle, walking up and down stairs alternating feet, and sliding down a slide at an accelerated pace. Throwing and catching skills are just beginning to emerge.

An important development in 2-year-olds is the emergence of constructive play. They love to make castles and cakes out of sand, packing sand into a mold, turning the mold upside down, and marveling at their creations. They are also learning to build towers and rows of blocks, to scribble with a crayon, and to propel a wheel toy across the floor.

The most remarkable developmental phenomenon at 2 years old is gaining the capacity to think in symbols. This new capacity manifests itself both in the emergence of pretend play and in the mastery of language. The 2-year-old represents thoughts and ideas in imitative actions, pretend play routines, and a rapidly growing vocabulary. While their pretend play is largely imitative, 2-year-olds are quite capable of acting out assumed roles or talking for miniature characters.

Three-Year-Olds

Three-year-olds have broadened their view of the world. Their ideas of time and place have undergone interesting transformations. They are beginning to grasp the complexities of their social world and to recognize the difference between real and pretend. Typical questions include "Where do birds sleep at night?" "Were there dinosaurs when you were a baby?" and "Are the people on television real or pretend?"

For these children, the past is divided into the immediate past, yesterday, last week and last month, and a long time ago, such as when their parents were young. The future is divided into tomorrow, soon, and "when I get big." Although they may not know the names of the seasons, 3-year-olds are beginning to make the relevant associations. They might remember summer as when it's hot and you go on vacation and fall as when the trees turn color, when you go trick-or-treating, and when you watch football on television.

Space, like time, is also divided into categories. Some places are near and you can walk to them. Some places are too far to walk. Some places are really far away, like Africa and the moon. There are also categories of people, such as children, teenagers, people who are old and work at jobs, and people who are very old and don't do much at all. Things can be living or not living, people and animals can be alive or dead, and things can be real or pretend.

By age 3½, the turbulence of the "terrible two's" has passed and a quieter child emerges. The 3-year-old is able to focus on a task for several minutes and to interact in a positive way with other children. By 3 years, children have expanded their repertoire of emotional responses. They can be sad or pensive. They can be jealous, wary, or frightened. They can be contented, jolly, or exuberant. They are also more tuned in to the feelings of others. Pleasing adults is becoming increasingly more important, and receiving praise or affection is becoming a powerful reinforcer. Although 3-year-olds are less apt to throw temper tantrums than 2-year-olds, their behavior can disintegrate when they are tired or hungry.

Four-Year-Olds

Four-year-old children are becoming increasingly aware of themselves as members of a peer group. Much of their day is spent establishing and maintaining their position with peers. Children who are 4 years old use their growing facility with words to praise or to criticize and correct other children, to call attention to their own accomplishments, and to convince a group to adopt their ideas. Four-year-olds are interested in playing with other children and will use threats and promises to win a friend or gain entry into a group. Remarks like "I'll be your best friend" and "I won't be your friend" are frequently heard in a preschool.

Out on the playground, 4-year-olds require plenty of space. They enjoy all varieties of play and are particularly fond of "monster" and "superhero" play.

Although 4-year-olds are learning to take turns and share toys, arguments over possessions take place continually. Frequently, disputes that begin verbally end with a push, a punch, or a skirmish. For the most part, the children do not really hurt each other in these skirmishes, but providing adult supervision is an important safeguard.

Four-year-olds love to learn new things, like pumping a swing, naming all the dinosaurs, counting up to 20, and playing games on the computer. They believe in what they see, hear, and touch. If a 4-year-old thinks his glass looks like it contains less juice than a friend's, then the friend has more juice, even if the juice was poured from two same-sized cans. If a 4-year-old heard a monster make growling noises under the bed, then there is a monster under the bed, even though his father says it's just his imagination. Four-year-olds are very curious, and their favorite word is likely to be *why*.

Five-Year-Olds

Five-year-olds seem older than 4-year-olds in many ways. Like 4-year-olds, 5-year-olds love to learn new things, but they are likely to be more persistent about mastery. If they are drawing a rainbow, a house, or a self-portrait, they will work for quite a while until it's just the way they want it to look. Like 4-year-olds, 5-year-olds love to pretend, but their pretending is more elaborate. They gather props before the pretending begins, and when they act out a pretend scene, the events take place in a logical sequence. If they are putting on a performance, they will set the stage, make the tickets, and put on their costumes before the performance begins. The performance is likely to include an announcement of what is going to happen, some sort of act or acts, and an elaborate ending with many bows and the expectation of applause.

Five-year-olds are interested in using and interpreting symbols. While some 5-year-olds are faster than others in learning the mechanics of reading and writing, most are serious about wanting to learn. They like to choose from a menu in the restaurant, read the signs on the road, make lists of things they need to buy, and write their names on their books or their drawings. They can work out simple problems in their heads and can grasp the concepts of adding and subtracting, although they are likely to count on their fingers before they come up with the right answer.

Five-year-olds who have the opportunity to use a computer love interactive programs. They are able to understand and apply the rules of a game and enjoy reading, writing, and number activities where the computer lets them know if they have the right answer. Favorite computer activities include programs that have them solve problems, programs that have them arrange characters on the screen to create their own imaginative stories, and programs that help them make drawings, paintings, birthday cards, and invitations.

Children at this age are quite likely to make playground plans before the day begins. Their choice of friends is likely to be made on the basis of shared interests. Children who like active play will choose to play on the climbing equipment, engage in running and chasing games, play some sort of ball game, or race around the playground on a vehicle. Children who like quieter play are more likely to play in the sand, hunt for bugs or lizards, put on a performance, or huddle with a friend and just talk.

Resources about Child Development

Berk, L. (2001). *Infants and children: Prenatal through middle childhood* (4th ed.). Upper Saddle River, NJ: Prentice Hall.

CDA Council for Professional Recognition. www.cdacouncil.org.

Zero to Three. National Center for Infants, Toddlers, and Families. www.zerotothree.org.

Health

Chapter 2

Overview

Often, we think of *health* as simply meaning the absence of disease. It is true that we can't stay healthy unless we learn good health habits that protect our bodies from illness, but we need to think of health in a larger sense. Being healthy means feeling fit and fine. It means having the internal resources to fight off illness and overcome the effects of physical insult; it also means having the energy and stamina to lead a productive life.

Rationale

Health is an important aspect of learning and development. Children who are healthy have the vigor they need for play, learning, and across-the-board development. Also, the more scientists learn about health, the more they become aware of the importance of behavior. Eating right, exercising, avoiding risks, practicing good hygiene and sanitation, and managing stress all contribute to long-term health. The habits acquired in early childhood tend to persist, so it is important to begin early with health education. In addition, nutritional deficits and toxic exposure in early childhood can cause wide-ranging, lifelong problems.

The early childhood teacher promotes health within the classroom by doing these things:

- Observing good health practices
- Conforming to the health rules and regulations of her center
- Recognizing the signs and symptoms of illness
- Developing a program of health education that teaches children to value good health and to follow the routines that maintain it

27

Objectives

1. To develop a sound knowledge base regarding health, nutrition, and oral hygiene

2. To carry out routine practices that will prevent illness and promote good health and nutrition

3. To establish guidelines/policies regarding how to handle health issues, including a record-keeping system

4. To incorporate activities that teach children and their families about health, oral/dental hygiene, and nutrition

5. To recognize indicators of abuse and/or neglect and follow the reporting policy mandated by the state

6. To keep oneself healthy and model appropriate wellness behaviors for children and their parents

Providing a Healthy Learning Environment

Mrs. Good-Care was washing out the bathroom sink when her assistant came into the room. "What are you doing?" she asked. "Just cleaning up the bathroom," Mrs. Good-Care explained. "The janitor didn't come in this morning." "That's ridiculous!" the assistant insisted. "Cleaning the bathroom is not *part of your job description."* ●

Like any good early childhood teacher, Mrs. Good-Care did not consult her job description before she cleaned the bathroom. She realized that she was responsible for the well-being of the children in her class, and she wasn't going to let a job description keep her from protecting their health.

In this chapter, we look at different ways in which classroom teachers safeguard the health of the children in their classes by updating their own health knowledge, maintaining a healthy environment, teaching children about health and nutrition, and recognizing and reporting child abuse and/or neglect.

To develop a sound knowledge base regarding health, nutrition, and oral hygiene

While classroom teachers are not expected to be physicians, they do need to know some fundamental concepts about health and nutrition. Most important, in order to safeguard the health and well-being of the children in your class, you need to be able to share information with parents. Your knowledge base should include the signs and symptoms of illness, recommended immunization timetables, and the daily nutritional needs of children under 6.

Before you focus on the knowledge about health issues related to child care, it is important to recognize the sequence of development relating to health and wellness (see the Developmental Picture below).

Developmental Picture

The young infant (0–9 months):

- Is dependent on others for meeting all basic needs
- Is likely to be alert and interactive during feeding and diapering
- Mouths objects to explore them

The caregiver:

- Helps infants establish a comfortable individual rhythm of sleeping, eating, waking, and playing
- Uses feeding and diapering times as opportunities to play and interact with babies
- Maintains routines for sanitary diapering, disinfecting mouthed toys, and washing bedding and clothing

The older infant (9–14 months):

- Is developing food preferences related to taste and texture and may push a spoon away
- Is interested in feeding himself and playing with food or throwing food on the floor
- Is learning from adult models
- Explores objects by touching, mouthing, and chewing on them

The caregiver:

- Provides time and support for practicing self-care tasks
- Provides finger foods and encourages children to feed themselves
- Is careful to offer nutritious food but not to force food
- Routinely cleans floors, equipment, and mouthed items
- Maintains sanitary diapering routines

The young toddler (14–24 months):

- Is not usually ready to be toilet trained
- Is likely to enjoy handwashing
- May be insistent about self-feeding
- Continues to explore objects with all senses, including taste

The caregiver:

- Does not expect toileting skills and maintains sanitary diapering routines
- Washes mouthed objects and maintains clean floors and play spaces
- Helps children wash their hands frequently
- Provides nutritious foods the child can eat easily with fingers or spoons in a relaxed atmosphere
- Does not force foods or insist that a child eat

(continued)

The older toddler (2 years):
- Is at a good age for toilet learning but may have accidents even when such learning has been achieved
- Enjoys being able to eat with a fork or spoon, wash her own hands, and brush her teeth with help
- Is anxious to do things all by himself
- Becomes listless or cranky and whiny when coming down with an illness

The caregiver:
- Makes toileting a routine activity for children who have begun toilet learning
- Makes sure every child has a change of clothes available
- Maintains a clean environment and washes toys after a child has mouthed them
- Recognizes signs of illness and separates the ill child from classmates

The preschool child (3–5 years):
- Is mastering self-care
- Is capable of learning good health habits
- Accomplishes independent eating, handwashing, toileting, toothbrushing, and nose wiping
- Is likely to be frightened of going to the doctor

The caregiver:
- Provides ample opportunities to develop body image, to practice self-care, and to develop good health habits
- Ensures children have nutritious foods, outdoor exercise, regular rest time, and a clean environment
- Isolates and sends home children with contagious diseases

Knowing the Signs and Symptoms of Illness

Some signs of illness, such as having a high fever and vomiting, are unmistakable, while other signs are more subtle and may be attributed to other causes. These signs and symptoms should be attended to:

Listlessness	Poor appetite
Inactivity	Urinating frequently
Moodiness	Tiring easily
Paleness	Deep circles under eyes
Excessive thirst	Chronic cough or runny nose
Difficulty with vision or hearing	Pink eyes
Hoarse voice	Nausea, vomiting, diarrhea
Skin rashes, crustiness, blotches	Complaints of headache, stiff neck, or other pain
Difficulty breathing	

Knowing about Contagious Diseases

Parents sometimes expect teachers to be all knowing. Although it is impossible to meet this kind of expectation, teachers should have a basic knowledge of the most common contagious diseases. They should also know how to obtain updated information from the local public health department, a pediatrician who consults to the center, and the Centers for Disease Control (www.cdc.gov).

Use the following chart to help you answer questions that parents might ask, like these:

> "My child was exposed to the measles last Saturday. If she is going to come down with the measles, when would she first show symptoms?"

Common Contagious Diseases

Disease	Incubation Period	When It Is "Catching"	Symptoms	Rash	Length of Illness	Prevention
Chicken pox	4–21 days	1 day before rash and 6 days after rash	Fever Rash Itching	Individual spots begin as water blisters, spread over whole body, form crusts by fourth day	7–10 days	Varicella
German measles	14–21 days	2 days before symptoms and 3 days after	Fever Slight cold Enlarged glands	First day: reddish-purple; Second day: Scarlet	3–5 days	M.M.R. vaccine
Measles	10–14 days	1 day before fever and until rash disappears	Fever Cough Conjunctivitis	Reddish-purple spots running into each other, from head downward	7–10 days	M.M.R. vaccine
Mumps	12–24 days	1 day before swelling and as long as swelling lasts	Fever Swelling under jaws	None	7–10 days	M.M.R. vaccine
Scarlet fever	2–7 days	From first symptoms until 7 days later	Fever Sore throat Headache Vomiting	Pinpoint scarlet rash on body, not on face	7–10 days	None
Whooping cough	7–14 days	From beginning of cough for 3–4 weeks	Cold Whooping cough Vomiting	None	4–6 weeks	D.P.T. vaccine

"My child has just had chicken pox. He's all better except for a couple of crusted-over spots on his forehead. Can he come back to school?"

"My child has a couple of red spots on her foot. Could that be the beginning of chicken pox?"

Use the next chart to help you answer the following questions that parents might ask about immunization:

"I went through the whole bit with shots and vaccinations when Theresa was a baby. She is turning 4 pretty soon. I don't need to do anything else, do I?"

"I think Marvin has had all of his shots. At least, they said he did at the health clinic when he was 6 months old. He's 18 months now. We just got back from a year in Uruguay. Does he need any kind of booster shots, or am I too late?"

Centers for Disease Control Immunization Guidelines (2004)

Disease and Vaccine	First Dose	Second Dose	Third Dose	Fourth Dose/ Boosters
Hepatitis B	At birth, if mother has been exposed; otherwise, 2–4 weeks	1–6 months	6–18 months	—
Diphtheria, Tetanus, Pertussis (DPT)	2 months	4 months	6 months	15–18 months, 4–6 years, then TD at 11–12 years and every 10 years thereafter
H. Influenza type B (HIB)	2 months	4 months	—	12 months or older
Polio (IPV)	2 months	4 months	6–18 months	4–6 years
Measles, Mumps, Rubella	12 months	4–6 years	—	—
Varicella (Chicken pox)	12 months if no history of chicken pox	—	—	—
Hepatitis A	2–12 years but only in high-risk geographic areas	—	—	—

Note: Any dose not given at the recommended age should be given as a catch-up immunization at any visit when indicated and feasible.

Source: www.cdc.gov. Approved by the Advisory Committee on Immunization Practices, the American Academy of Pediatrics, and the American Academy of Family Physicians. Note that the guidelines are reviewed every six months, so be sure to check for updates.

Conditions and Diseases That Are Common in a Child Care Setting

Additional information about the following diseases and conditions, as well as many others, can be found on the website of the national Centers for Disease Control (www.cdc.gov).

Head Lice

Signs and Symptoms: Intense itching. Nits are most often found in the hair at the nape of the neck and over the ears.

Incubation Period: Retreatment is generally recommended 7–10 days after the first application due to the hatching of more nits.

Treatment: A special shampoo, available over the counter or by a doctor's prescription. Removal of the nits with the use of a fine-toothed comb.

Mode of Transmission: A parasite that is passed from person to person via personal items such as hats and combs.

Prevention: Do not allow children to share items that touch the hair, such as hats and combs. Clean rugs and bedding frequently.

Pink Eye (Conjunctivitis)

Signs and Symptoms: Red, watery eyes, discharge, crusty eyes, sensitivity to light.

Incubation Period: Usually 24–72 hours.

Treatment: Antibiotic (through a doctor's prescription).

Mode of Transmission: Through contact with eye discharge.

Prevention: Avoid touching the eyes. Practice frequent handwashing. Wash towels and bedding. Avoid sharing of these items.

Impetigo

Signs and Symptoms: Flat, yellow, crusty, or weeping patch on the skin.

Incubation Period: 5 days.

Treatment: Washing of infected areas with mild soap and water. Doctor may prescribe an antibiotic or ointment.

Mode of Transmission: The infected person can easily spread the infection to other parts of his own body and to others by direct contact.

Prevention: Bathe daily with a mild soap. Keep hands and fingernails clean. Practice frequent handwashing.

Pin Worms (Seat Worms)

Signs and Symptoms: Tiny, white worms that cause itching and irritation of the anus.

Incubation Period: After swallowing the eggs, it takes from 15–28 days for the worms to mature.

Treatment: Consult a physician.

Mode of Transmission: The eggs are passed from the anus to the mouth. Children scratch the affected area where the eggs are, and the eggs then lodge under the fingernails.

Prevention: Practice frequent handwashing and proper diapering and toileting procedures.

Common Cold

Signs and Symptoms: Runny nose, watery eyes, sore throat, chills and malaise (blah feeling). Usually no fever unless complication has developed.

Incubation Period: 12–72 hours. Usually 24 hours.

Treatment: No specific treatment. Treat the symptoms to make the infected person feel better. Rest. Drink plenty of fluids.

Mode of Transmission: Through direct contact with coughs and sneezes and indirectly through contaminated surfaces, hands, and articles such as tissues.

Prevention: Wash hands. Cover coughs and sneezes. Dispose of tissues properly. Wash surfaces and toys frequently.

Ear Infection (Otitis-Media)

Signs and Symptoms: Pain, drainage from the ears, red ears, fever, tugging at the ears, irritability.

Incubation Period: Several days to several months.

Treatment: Consult a physician. Chronic infections may be treated with the surgical placement of tubes so that the ears can drain.

Mode of Transmission: Virus or bacterial infection. Upper-respiratory infections are usually spread by coughs and sneezes. Sometimes antibiotics are given. Some doctors have a wait-and-see attitude.

Prevention: Cover sneezes and coughs. Practice frequent handwashing and disinfecting of surfaces and toys.

Respiratory Syncytial Virus (RSV)

Signs and Symptoms: Similar to common cold. May result in lower-respiratory tract infections or otitis-media. Especially seen in toddlers younger than 18 months.

Incubation Period: Contagious before symptoms appear to 1–3 weeks after symptoms subside.

Treatment: Symptoms are treated. Severe cases may require hospitalization.

Mode of Transmission: Spread through direct contact with infectious secretions.

Prevention: Practice frequent handwashing, cleaning, and disinfecting of surfaces and toys.

Diarrhea (Rotavirus)

Signs and Symptoms: Loose, watery stools, abdominal cramps, sometimes a runny nose and cough.

Incubation Period: 2 days.

Treatment: Rest and a bland diet, avoidance of dairy products, plenty of fluids to reduce the chance of dehydration.

Mode of Transmission: Through the fecal/oral route.

Prevention: Practice frequent handwashing. Disinfect surfaces and toys.

Salmonella

Signs and Symptoms: Diarrhea, flulike symptoms, stomach cramping, vomiting.

Incubation Period: Several days to several months.

Treatment: Usually no specific treatment. Severe cases should seek a doctor's advice.

Mode of Transmission: Eating of infected foods, cross-contamination of foods, handling of reptiles such as iguanas and turtles.

Prevention: Ensure the proper preparation, cooking, handling, and storage of food. Practice proper handwashing after handling reptiles and other pets.

Fifth Disease

Signs and Symptoms: A "slapped face" rash. Fever and flulike symptoms. The rash spreads to the trunk and extremities and may cause itching.

Incubation Period: Usually 4–14 days but can be as long as 20 days. Most contagious before symptoms appear.

Treatment: No specific treatment.

Mode of Transmission: By direct contact with respiratory secretions and airborne droplets.

Prevention: Wash hands after touching any secretions from the nose or mouth.

Hand–Foot–Mouth Disease (Coxsackie Virus)

Signs and Symptoms: Canker sore–like sores in the mouth and a rash on the bottoms of the feet, the palms of the hands, and sometimes the buttocks. A sore throat and mild fever.

Incubation Period: Usually 3–6 days. Most infectious for 7 days after development of the rash.

Treatment: No specific treatment.

Mode of Transmission: Through the fecal/oral route or through respiratory secretions.

Prevention: Practice frequent handwashing and good personal hygiene.

Hepatitis B (HBV)

Signs and Symptoms: Fatigue, loss of appetite, jaundice, dark urine, light stools, nausea, vomiting, abdominal pain.

Incubation Period: Around 3 months.

Treatment: No specific treatment.

Mode of Transmission: Infected mother to newborn through blood exposure at birth, or through exposure of cuts or mucous membranes to contaminated blood.

Prevention: Practice frequent handwashing. Clean up and disinfect blood spills immediately, and wear gloves. Do not share toothbrushes.

Strep Throat

Signs and Symptoms: Sore throat, sometimes a fever and tiredness. A rash may also appear. Swollen tonsils and lymph glands.

Incubation Period: 1–3 days.

Treatment: Doctor's prescription of antibiotics.

Mode of Transmission: Contact with infected person.

Prevention: Isolation of infected person for at least 24 hours after starting antibiotics.

Chicken Pox

Signs and Symptoms: Virus and a slight fever. Blisters that first appear on the face, the back, under the arms, and the "hot spots" on the body.

Incubation Period: 2–3 weeks. No longer contagious as soon as all of the lesions have crusted over and the sores are not wet or weeping.

Treatment: There is a vaccine for chicken pox. If children do get chicken pox, a fever-reducing medicine is usually suggested by a physician. Do *not* give aspirin, which can cause Reyes syndrome.

Mode of Transmission: Respiratory. Contact with an infected person. Hands and surfaces that are contaminated through sneezing and coughing discharges, as well as airborne germs through the same transmission.

Prevention: Again, there is a vaccine. An infected person should be isolated for at least 24 hours after starting medicine.

Bottle Mouth

Signs and Symptoms: Tooth decay.

Treatment: See a dentist.

Mode of Transmission: Infants' and toddlers' teeth are exposed to surgery liquids, formula, milk, and juices.

Prevention: Do not let an infant/toddler go to sleep with a bottle in his or her mouth; wean from bottle at 12 months. Do not let an infant/toddler carry a bottle around in his or her mouth.

Knowing about Nutrition

Mrs. Easy-Going was talking with her 4-year-old's teacher. "My Melissa is a very fussy eater," she explained. "Like most 4-year-olds, she hates fruits and vegetables. She also hates meat, milk, cheese, yogurt, and cereal. But don't worry if she doesn't eat lunch at school. I always stop on the way to school to buy her hash browns, and we get a big bag of french fries on the way home. She's perfectly healthy, and I don't want to make a big deal about food." "Is she allergic to anything?" the teacher asked. "No," said Mrs. Easy-Going, "she has no allergies. She just knows what she likes and what she hates."

Melissa's teacher assured Mrs. Easy-Going that she would not force Melissa to eat anything she did not want. True to her word, Melissa's teacher did not make a fuss over Melissa's lunch. She served Melissa a small portion of the school lunch every day and explained to Melissa that she could eat as much or as little as she wanted. When Mrs. Easy-Going came to visit her daughter at lunch one day, she was surprised to find her eating a cheeseburger with a glass of milk. "I thought you hated cheeseburgers," Mrs. Easy-Going commented to Melissa. "I do," Melissa replied, "except I like the way they make them at school."

Melissa's teacher was concerned about providing her preschool children with a well-balanced and nutritional meal. At the same time, she respected Mrs. Easy-Going's child-rearing philosophy and agreed not to pressure Melissa into eating. She served Melissa a small portion of a well-balanced lunch on a daily basis and gradually introduced new foods to her.

Meeting Young Children's Nutritional Needs

Proper nutrition is very important for young children. They are growing rapidly, and they need adequate amounts of protein, carbohydrates, fats, vitamins, and minerals in order to stay healthy. Vitamin C, iron, protein, and calcium are especially important, and some children do not get adequate amounts of these essential nutrients.

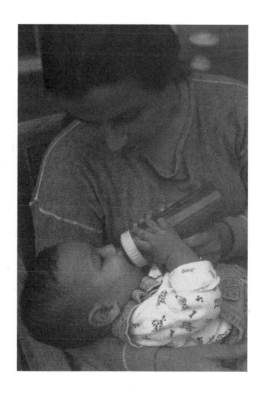

Foods rich in Vitamin C include tomatoes, broccoli, cabbage, peppers, strawberries, kiwi fruit, cantaloupe, and citrus fruits, such as oranges, tangerines, and grapefruit. High-protein foods include soy, lean meats, beans and other legumes, nuts, eggs, and fish. Dairy foods are high in both protein and calcium. Foods rich in iron include meat, eggs, legumes, spinach and other leafy greens, dried fruits (e.g., prunes, apricots, and raisins), and whole-grain and cereal products that have been enriched with iron.

The toddler and preschool years are also the time when eating habits are established. Although all children develop personal likes and dislikes, they also take cues from those around them. If a toddler sees others enjoying vegetables, she is likely to think they are tasty. If junk food is the norm at the child's home and child care setting, he may develop poor habits that are hard to break.

The U.S. Department of Agriculture (USDA) provides food guides to help Americans set nutritional goals and to promote overall health. These guidelines cover such issues as how much protein should be consumed each day; how much fat or sugar is too much; what counts as a serving of fruits, vegetables, whole grains, or dairy; and how many servings of each are recommended. The guidelines are revised every five years to reflect new research and to make sure that they are clear and easy to follow. The most recent dietary guidelines describe a healthy diet as one with these characteristics:

- Emphasizes fruits, vegetables, whole grains, and low-fat milk products
- Includes lean meats, poultry, fish, beans, eggs, and nuts
- Is low in saturated fats, trans fats, cholesterol, salt, and added sugars

Food groups are defined to help people determine what goes into a balanced diet. They include the following:

- *Breads and other cereals*—breads, pasta, rice, cereals
- *Fruits*—apples, pears, oranges, peaches, bananas, pineapples
- *Vegetables*—peas, carrots, broccoli, collard greens, sweet potatoes, beans, corn
- *Meats and other proteins*—beef, poultry, fish, dry beans, eggs, nuts
- *Milk products*—milk, yogurt, cheese
- *Fats*, *oils*, *sweets*—butter, soy margarine, chocolate, candies, sodas

The USDA also publishes materials for specific populations, such as guides for young children, vegetarians, people with particular religious requirements or cultural preferences, and people with food allergies and other special dietary needs.

The most up-to-date information can be found on the USDA website (www.usda.gov/FoodAndNutrition). Kid-friendly recipes for nutritious meals and snacks, tips for cooking with young children, age-appropriate teaching activities, and other resources can be found at www.nal.usda.gov/childcare.

The USDA also operates several programs to help low-income individuals and families meet their nutritional needs. As a teacher or caregiver of young children, you should be informed about two such programs in particular:

- The Special Supplemental Nutrition Program for Women, Infants, and Children, better known as the *WIC Program*, helps to safeguard the health of low-income women, infants, and children up to age 5 by providing nutritious foods to supplement their diets, information on healthy eating, and referrals to health care. See www.fns.usda.gov/wic for information on how families can access these services.

- The Child and Adult Care Food Program (CACFP) is funded by the federal government and administered by state agencies. It helps child care providers—including centers, Head Start programs, family child care homes, and school-age programs—to purchase nutritious meals. Providers can receive various levels of reimbursement for meal purchases, depending on the percentage of children they serve whose family incomes make them eligible for free or reduced lunch or other federal subsidies. For agency contacts in your state, see www.fns.usda.gov/cnd/Contacts/StateDirectory.htm.

Providing a Pleasant Environment during Meals and Snacks

- Bottle feeding provides a special opportunity to hold a child in your lap and encourage closeness. Never prop the bottle.
- In some child care centers, family-style serving (having the children select from serving bowls) is preferred. In other centers, particularly those where children bring in their own meals, each child is served individually. Family style extends the time it takes to have a meal and, at the same time, provides opportunities to use utensils and to have the children talk about the food with their caregivers.
- Have a comfortable conversation with the children as they are having their meal.
- Try not to rush the children or leave them at the table too long.

Presenting Meals to Children That Take into Account Their Age and Readiness

- Mealtime provides an opportunity to help children develop self-help skills.
- Encourage children to use the appropriate utensils and cups.
- Young toddlers can learn to use a spoon and drink from a "tippy" cup.
- Older toddlers can learn to use a fork with rounded tines and to drink from a cup with handles.
- Preschool-age children can learn to use a dull knife and to drink from a glass.
- Provide activities that allow children to help with simple food preparation. Some examples include helping to set the table, pouring their drinks from small pitchers, and spreading cream cheese, hummus, or salsa on a bagel, pita, or tortilla.

Avoiding Foods That Could Endanger Children's Health

- Avoid foods that could cause choking. Children 5 years old and under should not be given foods that they could choke on, such as hotdogs, undiced carrots, and whole grapes.
- Avoid foods that could be aspirated or sucked into the lungs. Children 5 years old and under should not be given foods such as popcorn and nuts.

Recognizing That Some Children May Have Food Allergies or Sensitivities

- Maintain a list of children with food allergies and other allergies.
- As you plan menus and cooking projects, consult the food allergy list.
- Know how each individual child's allergy manifests itself and what to do in case of accidental exposure.

Involving Parents in Nutrition

- If parents provide snacks and/or meals, provide a list of suggestions to help them select nutritious foods.
- Provide parents with a list of appropriate and inappropriate foods to bring into the classroom for special events.
- Provide parents with a list of healthy snacks that they can give their children, such as the following:

Cheese	Bananas
Cooked carrot rounds	Whole-wheat crackers
Orange sections	Cheerios
Cooked or frozen peas	Yogurt
String cheese	Rice pudding
Cottage cheese	Quesadillas
Cut-up grapes	Cherry tomato halves
Hard-boiled eggs	Tofu squares
Thinly sliced or diced apples, pears, or peaches	

Promoting Good Oral Hygiene

Oral hygiene is another important health topic:

- Provide healthy foods for teeth, including calcium-rich foods like milk and crunchy foods like apples.
- Limit the amounts of sugary, sweet, and sticky foods.
- Explain to parents that leaving a bottle in an infant's crib while she is falling asleep is likely to produce "bottle mouth," or rot a baby's teeth.

To carry out routine practices that will prevent illness and promote good health and nutrition

The health practices that are most important for controlling the spread of disease in a classroom include the following:

- Following universal precautions
- Washing hands
- Washing and disinfecting surfaces
- Following appropriate procedures when changing diapers
- Maintaining a healthy indoor environment

Following Universal Precautions

Universal precautions is the term used to identify a set of strategies designed to protect people from infections that are spread through contact with blood and other bodily fluids. These guidelines should be followed without exception in child care settings, both for the protection of the caregiver and for the protection of the children:

- Avoid direct contact with bodily fluids, including blood, urine, feces, vomit, saliva, and nasal/eye discharge.
- Use disposable gloves in these situations:
  — When handling body fluids
  — When handling food
  — When helping a child in the bathroom
  — When changing a diaper
- Clean up and disinfect any bodily fluid spills immediately.
- Avoid any contact with sources of bodily fluids, such as the eyes, nose, mouth, and open sores.
- Discard contaminated material in a tightly secured plastic bag.

Using Appropriate Handwashing Procedures

Staff in child care centers should wash their hands in these situations using the sequence outlined in the box on page 50:

- When arriving at work
- Before leaving for the day
- Before preparing and/or serving food or bottles
- Before and after diapering a child or helping a child in the bathroom
- After cleaning up body fluids
- After wiping a child's nose
- When coming in from the playground
- After handling pets
- After tying shoes
- When hands look dirty
- After coughing or sneezing
- After personal toileting

Handwashing Sequence

- Gather all of the materials necessary.
- Remove jewelry. (When possible, avoid wearing jewelry when working with children.)
- Use soap and running water.
- Rub hands vigorously as you wash them.
- Wash the backs of the hands, the palms, the wrists, between the fingers, and under the fingernails.
- Rinse your hands well and leave the water running.
- Dry your hands with a paper or single-use towel.
- Turn off the water by using a paper towel, not your bare hands.

Activities for Engaging Children in Handwashing

The procedure for washing hands for children and adults is the same. The problem is that children aren't very good at judging how long to keep their hands under the water in order to rinse well. It also takes children time and practice to remember the sequence for washing hands.

The following activities provide ways of helping children learn handwashing techniques:

Handwashing Song Sing this handwashing song with the appropriate motions (to the tune of "All around the Mulberry Bush").

> *This is the way I turn on the faucet,*
> *Turn on the faucet, turn on the faucet.*
> *This is the way I turn on the faucet,*
> *Early in the morning.*

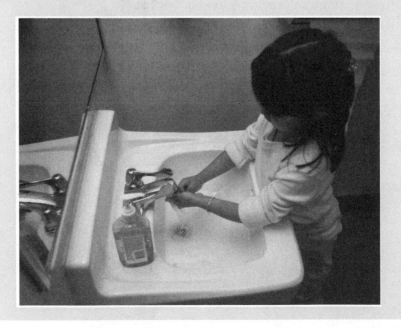

This is the way I lather my hands, etc.
This is the way I scrub my hands, etc.
This is the way I rinse my hands, etc.
This is the way I dry my hands, etc.
This is the way I turn off the faucet, etc.

"Oops—I Forgot!" Game Pantomime the sequence on handwashing. Leave out one step, and see if the children can tell you what is missing.

Sequence Cards Buy or create your own set of sequence cards on handwashing. Let children arrange the cards in order, or put the cards in the wrong order and let the children correct your mistake. Omit one card, and see if the children can tell you what is missing. Put up handwashing sequence cards in the bathroom to serve as a reminder.

Doll Bath Set up a doll bath in the classroom. Then give a doll a bath in front of the children. Talk to the doll about the importance of washing its face first or making sure that you wash between the toes and so on. Give the children a chance to wash the doll, praising them for remembering the correct order and for making sure all parts get cleaned.

Cleaning and Disinfecting the Room and Materials

The director of Safeguard Child Care Center was taking new parents around to see the facility. "What makes our school so special," the director explained, "is the professionalism of our staff. We are very proud of the fact that our teachers are given job descriptions that recognize that teaching children is a full-time job. We have a secretary to manage the office, a bus driver to drive the bus, a cook to make the meals, and a custodian who comes in after school to clean up the classroom. Our teachers are not expected to wipe down the shelves or wash off toys that babies have used."

The director was sure that all the parents on her tour would be impressed with her personnel policies. However, several of the parents were upset by her comments and began asking questions:

- *What happens if a child messes up the floor in the middle of the day when the custodian isn't around?*
- *What happens if babies put toys in their mouths?*
- *Who is responsible for cleaning off the tables before and after snack-time?*

Although the director thought that she was just being considerate of her staff when she relieved them of clean-up duty, it was easy for the parents to recognize that the children were being placed at risk.

Cleaning up in an early childhood classroom is an ongoing responsibility that everyone must share. Messes must be cleaned up when they are made. Toys must be cleaned after they have been mouthed.

Here is a short poem about cleaning that will help you to remember the quick and easy solution to the clean-up problems you will face during a normal day:

> *Keep out germs. Cut down on pollution.*
> *Spray every day with a fresh bleach solution.*
> *Mix water (1 gallon) with bleach (/ cup).*
> *The sick rate will go down and attendance will go up!*

Here are more guidelines for cleaning solutions:

- Make a fresh bleach solution every day (/ cup bleach to 1 gallon water).
- Dispense the bleach solution from a spray bottle.
- On a daily basis, disinfect all tabletops and toys that have been mouthed.

Practicing Appropriate Diapering Procedures

Using appropriate diapering procedures, as described in the box below, is another important health practice.

Diapering Sequence

- Have needed supplies ready, including a clean diaper, clothing, towelettes, and any creams or lotions that you are using with the child.
- Be sure that the diaper-changing surface is washable and nonporous.
- Place a fresh piece of paper on the changing area. It is important to change the paper after each diaper change.
- Put on gloves.
- Place the child on the changing table. Remember to keep one hand on the child at all times.
- Remove the soiled diaper.
- Clean the child with towelettes, wiping from front to back.
- Dispose of the soiled diaper and towelettes in a plastic-lined container.
- Remove your gloves and dispose of them in the container.
- Put on a clean diaper and dress the child.
- Wash the child's hands.
- Return the child to a safe area.
- Place any soiled clothing in a plastic bag to give to the parent.
- Remove the changing table paper and discard it, remembering to only touch clean areas of the paper.
- Clean and disinfect the diaper-changing area.
- Wash your hands thoroughly with soap and hot water, using appropriate handwashing techniques.

Use diapering time to carry on a playful conversation with the child.

Maintaining a Healthy Indoor Environment

Follow these suggestions for providing a healthy indoor environment:

- Keep the air in the room fresh by opening windows, if possible.
- Make outdoor activities part of the daily schedule.
- Alternate quiet times and physical activity to keep children active, alert, and healthy and to provide a time for children to rest or sleep.
- Provide space between children's mats, cots, and cribs to reduce the spread of respiratory infections.
- Check state and local rules and regulations for additional requirements, such as lead-free certification, ventilation requirements, and pest-control guidelines.

To establish guidelines/policies regarding how to handle health issues, including a record-keeping system

Establishing guidelines and keeping accurate records is also important to ensuring a healthy environment.

Maintaining Health and Immunization Records for Every Child

- The Centers for Disease Control (CDC) publishes annually a recommended immunization chart that lists the types of immunizations required by law and the ages when initial immunization and booster shots are required. You should have verification of up-to-date immunization for every child or a note from a physician stating the reason that the child has not been vaccinated.
- Require that verification of physicals be updated, as required by the state and local enforcement agencies.
- Develop a system for maintaining physical and immunization records for children and a system of informing parents when they need to update immunizations and/or physicals.
- Maintain a health record for each child that includes comments from the daily health check, any unusual incidences or concerns, height and weight, alternative food plans, and allergic reactions.

Knowing the Guidelines Set By Your Center for Excusing Children from Child Care Due to Illness

Centers need to develop policies indicating when mildly ill children can and cannot attend child care. Many children with mild illnesses can safely attend the center. Be sure to share these guidelines with parents. Also, know when to report communicable diseases and other conditions to the health department.

Objective 4 To incorporate activities that teach children and families about health, oral/dental hygiene, and nutrition

When we think about all the different things we would like young children to know about health and nutrition, it is difficult to know what to emphasize or even where to begin. One possible way to start is to make a list of some of the basic concepts you would like children to learn in the course of the year. Next, develop lesson plans devoted to these concepts. You might want to do a theme or unit near the beginning of the year or offer brief lessons on a weekly basis.

Basic Concepts about Health and Wellness Appropriate for Preschool Children

- Our bodies get strong when we get to sleep on time, get a lot of fresh air, and eat healthy foods.
- Germs make us sick. When we wash our hands before we eat and after we go to the bathroom, we get rid of germs.
- Germs spread when we sneeze or cough. That's why we need to cover our mouths with our hands when we sneeze or cough and then wash our hands.
- Cigarettes are not good for our bodies.
- We brush our teeth at least twice a day to keep them clean and healthy.

Basic Concepts about Nutrition

- Eating the right kinds of food makes us strong and healthy.
- Foods like candy and sweetened cereal are bad for our teeth.

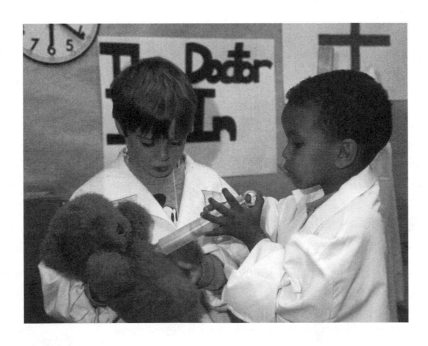

- Foods that are high in protein—such as meat, fish, beans, and cheese—make us strong and give us energy.
- Eating a lot of fruits and vegetables gives us vitamins that keep us feeling well.

Activities for Learning about Nutrition

Pretend Play

Objective: To teach children to recognize healthy foods

Procedure: Set up a "restaurant" in your classroom. Provide appropriate props, such as chef hats, aprons, menus, trays, pads and pencils, pretend food, napkins, place settings, and a cash register. Join the play as the "waitress" or the "parent," so that you can talk about ordering healthy foods.

Food Books

Objective: To teach children about the different food groups

Procedure: Help children construct their own food books by cutting pictures of foods out of newspapers and magazines or using labels from food packaging. Make separate pages or books for breads and cereals, dairy products, meats and other proteins, fruits, and vegetables.

Basic Concepts about Dental Care

- Brushing our teeth after every meal keeps them strong and healthy.
- The dentist is a special kind of doctor who helps us take care of our teeth.

Activity for Learning about Dental Care

No-Cavities Collages

Objective: To teach children oral hygiene

Procedure: Draw a smiling face on one piece of tagboard and a sad face on another. Ask children to bring in magazine pictures and wrappers that represent foods that are good for your teeth and foods that are not good for your teeth. Let the children paste things that are good for your teeth on the "happy face" tagboard, such as a picture of an orange, and things that are bad for your teeth on the "sad face" tagboard, such as a candy wrapper or the top from a box of highly sugared cereal.

To recognize indicators of abuse and/or neglect and follow the reporting policy mandated by the state

Child abuse and neglect is a national problem. Maltreatment, according to long-term studies, is associated with dropping out of school, committing violent crimes, and being unemployed. There is also evidence that children who have been abused are at risk for becoming child abusers when they become parents.

Every child care provider is required by state law to report suspected abuse. If you suspect that a child in your center has been abused, follow the procedures for reporting set by your center. If you are a family child care provider, report directly to the abuse hotline in your state. Familiarize yourself with the indicators of abuse described in the following child maltreatment chart.

Types of Child Maltreatment

Type of Abuse or Neglect	Physical Indicators	Behavioral Indicators
Physical abuse	• Unexplained bruises, welts, burns, fractures, lacerations, and abrasions	• Afraid of adults • Afraid of parents and/or to go home • Anxious about routine activities, like sleeping, eating, and toileting • Can be either aggressive or withdrawn
Emotional abuse	• Failure to thrive • Lags behind other children in physical development • Developmental delays	• Habit disorders (sucking, biting, rocking) • Withdrawn or aggressive • Poor peer relations
Sexual abuse	• Difficulty walking or sitting • Bloody underclothes • Bruises or bleeding in genitalia, vaginal, or rectal areas • Venereal disease or pregnancy (with teens) • Wears clothing and/or makeup beyond his or her years	• Unwilling to take off clothing • Unusual sexual behavior or knowledge of sexual behavior beyond what children his or her age should know • Poor peer and adult relations
Neglect	• Poor hygiene • Inappropriate dress • Medical needs are not met • Lack of supervision • Abandonment • Always hungry	• Begging, stealing food, or taking food from the trash • Asks to take food home • Arrives early and is picked up late • Constant fatigue or falls asleep in class • Withdrawn

objective 6
To keep oneself healthy and model appropriate wellness behaviors for children and their parents

Miss It's-My-Business was called into the office by the director of the center.

Director: "I heard that you had a great meeting last night with your parent volunteer group."

Miss It's-My-Business: "They're a fabulous group of parents, and we made some really exciting plans."

Director: "There is just one thing that concerns me. One of the parents said that when you went out for coffee after the meeting, you were smoking nonstop and—"

Miss It's-My-Business (interrupting): "I never smoke at school, and I don't appreciate your telling me what I should do after school! If I want to ruin my health, I'll do what I please. It's my health."

Director: "I wasn't trying to interfere with what you do in your spare time. It's just that I would like to see you take better care of yourself. Remember, last year, you had three attacks of bronchitis."

Although Miss It's-My-Business was miffed when the director commented on her smoking, the director made a valid point. It is important for all child caregivers to maintain their own health.

Most of us are fully aware of how to take care of our health:

- Eat nutritious meals.
- Maintain the weight level recommended for your height and body build.
- Get an annual physical and regular dental check-ups.
- Get prenatal care in the first trimester of pregnancy.
- Get enough rest and exercise, and avoid getting overstressed.
- Abstain from smoking, abusing alcohol, and taking illegal drugs.
- Make sure your immunizations are up to date. Also ask your health provider if an annual flu shot is advisable.

Unfortunately, the easy part is *knowing* how to stay healthy. The hard part is making a commitment to wellness and living up to that commitment.

> *Unfortunately, the easy part is* knowing *how to stay healthy. The hard part is making a commitment to wellness and living up to that commitment.*

One way to convert your good intentions for maintaining a healthy lifestyle into commitment is to recognize the benefits that desirable health practices provide:

- When we feel good, we are happier, more energetic, and better at coping with minor problems.
- If we "practice what we preach," we are good models for children and parents. When Miss It's-My-Business smoked in a coffeehouse with parents from her center, she was sending a message that it is okay for adults to smoke when they are not in the child care facility.
- When we are committed to wellness, we are more likely to have a better attendance record at work. If we ever want to change jobs or advance our careers, letters of recommendation that include a good record of attendance are bound to be helpful.
- Staying healthy is cost effective. The cost of medical care continues to rise, so in a very literal sense, it pays to stay healthy.

You should have health insurance. If you are an independent provider or if your center does not offer insurance coverage, investigate state programs. Your local child care professional organization, union, or resource and referral agency may be able to help you locate resources for obtaining medical insurance.

Additional Resources about Health

Aronson, S. (2002). *Healthy young children: A manual for programs* (4th ed.). Washington, DC: NAEYC.

Caring for Our Children—National health and safety performance standards: Guidelines for out of home child care programs (2nd ed). (2002). Washington, DC: NAEYC. (Updated standards issued jointly by the American Academy of Pediatrics, American Public Health Association, and the National Resource Center for Health and Safety in Child Care)

Centers for Disease Control (CDC). www.cdc.gov.

Learning Environments

Chapter 3

Overview

A learning environment for preschool children is a place that is conducive to learning and appropriate for the developmental levels and learning characteristics of the children.

Rationale

The arrangement of a classroom or family child care setting sets the tone for learning. The selection and setup of play materials, the pictures on the walls, and even the way the room is divided all support beliefs about what and how children should learn. For example, placing puzzles and sorting toys on low shelves invites children to learn mathematical concepts through play. Creating a pretend play area that can become a "fire station," "circus tent," or "café" invites children to learn about their world by playing together. On the other hand, setting desks in rows and keeping materials on high shelves suggest that learning is controlled by the teacher and that children should not explore on their own or learn from each other.

Preschoolers need an environment that is safe and welcoming, intriguing but not overwhelming. In a well-planned environment, babies will spend less time crying and more time exploring. Older children will spend less time wandering, fidgeting, and fighting and more time asking questions, working together, and mastering new skills.

Objectives

1. To set up an environment that takes into account the behavioral characteristics, needs, and interests of infants at different stages (0–14 months)

2. To set up an environment that takes into account the behavioral characteristics, needs, and interests of young toddlers (14–24 months)

3. To set up an environment that takes into account the behavioral characteristics, needs, and interests of older toddlers (2 years)

4. To organize and equip a preschool classroom that promotes different kinds of play and learning experiences and that reflects the interests, needs, ability levels, and family backgrounds of the children (3–5 years)

5. To organize and equip a learning environment for a multiage or family child care setting that includes children ages birth through 5

6. To develop a well-balanced daily schedule

7. To set up an outdoor play and learning environment

8. To ensure that the learning environment works for adults as well as for children

Providing a Developmentally Appropriate Learning Environment

The chair of the parent advisory board from the Key to Growth Child Care Center arrived in the director's office full of excitement. "I just received the most wonderful news," the chair reported. "The Tot Toy Factory has agreed to give us the most fabulous contribution. They are giving us their complete display of oversized cardboard Sesame Street characters. This place will look great with a giant Muppet in every classroom!"

The director of the center was in a quandary. On the one hand, she wanted to be gracious and accept this gift with enthusiasm. On the other hand, she wasn't so sure that her teachers would welcome the giant Muppets. They were too big to fit into a classroom without rearranging the learning centers. Thinking quickly, she came up with a perfect solution. "I am so appreciative of all that you have done for this center. You are always thinking of us. Instead of putting one Muppet in each classroom, why don't we line them all up on the way out to the playground? They'll be a real conversation piece for the children."

The director didn't want to give up either her belief in the importance of parent participation or her belief in setting up an environment that expressed the philosophy of active learning that was so important to her and to her teachers. Fortunately, she found a quick solution that was consistent with both.

To set up an environment that takes into account the behavioral characteristics, needs, and interests of infants at different stages (0–14 months)

Ms. Shipshape had the infant room just the way she liked it. The cribs were lined up in a row on one side. The rattles were in a box that she could reach without stooping. The floor was clear. The walls were gleaming white. There wasn't a pillow in sight. Everything had been disinfected.

"This is no place for a baby," said Mrs. Earthmother when she came to visit. "It's too sterile!" ●

Ms. Shipshape and Mrs. Earthmother each have a point. Babies do need an environment that is easy to keep sanitary. They also need to be in a space that is cozy, that looks and feels like home, and that provides them with interesting things to look at and inviting places to explore. As described in the Developmental Picture on page 62, infants have specific interests as well as needs.

Basic Considerations for Setting Up an Infant Room

Consider the following in deciding how to set up an infant room:

- *Infants spend much of the day sleeping.* The infant room should have a sleeping room or area with a crib for every child.

- *During their periods of wakefulness, infants learn best from their interactions with adults.* The infant room should have well-equipped areas for changing and feeding that encourage adult/infant interaction.

- *During their wakeful periods, infants learn from playing with a variety of toys.* Teachers should be sure that every infant, when awake, has age-appropriate toys to play with.

- *Infants as young as 6 months old enjoy interaction with other infants.* The infant room should have a safe and easily cleaned area where two or three infants can play together.

- *The needs and schedules for an infant may change on a daily basis.* Every infant room should have a bulletin board where emergency telephone numbers, schedules, and instructions from parents are posted.

- *Infants are vulnerable to contagious illnesses and to overstimulation.* If there are more than 8 to 10 children in a room, it should be divided into two or more areas so that there are never more than 10 bodies in a room together.

Equipping the Infant Room

Sleeping Area

An infant room must have one crib for every infant, but finding room for cribs can be a challenge. Some people solve the problem by putting the cribs on wheels and moving them aside when they are not in use. Others use the spaces under cribs for storage.

When in use, cribs should be at least 18 inches apart and should be arranged so that the supervisor has full view of every infant. See-through cribs let caregivers look in and babies look out.

Generally, infants should have a separate area for sleeping, where the light and noise levels can be kept low. When a separate space is not available, use room dividers to create a quiet corner. A rocking chair in the sleeping area is useful for comforting fussy babies.

Developmental Picture

The young infant (0–9 months):

- Is limited in mobility
- Is attracted to interesting sights, sounds, and objects and enjoys watching people
- Has individual needs for sleeping and eating
- Is likely to be startled or overstimulated by a sudden noise or a room that is noisy, very bright, or filled with activity
- May "tune out," fuss, fall asleep, or be unable to sleep when overstimulated
- May fuss or cry when bored
- Needs to spend some playtime on his stomach on a firm surface to learn to roll over, crawl, and get into a sitting position

The caregiver:

- Provides a variety of perspectives by moving the infant about
- Brings experiences to the infant to look at, listen to, and touch
- Recognizes that infants have different levels of tolerance in terms of sound and visual stimulation and reads each child's cues
- Separates young infants from more active playmates
- Provides a quiet sleeping area
- Follows the infant's feeding and sleeping schedule, moving toward a regular rhythm

The older infant (9–14 months):

- Is creeping, cruising, and learning to walk and may be practicing walking and climbing skills
- Has favorite toys and is interested in selecting her own toys
- Enjoys emptying and filling and holding soft cuddly things
- Is interested in exploring new spaces
- Can suddenly become overtired and/or overstimulated

The caregiver:

- Provides space and equipment for active movement indoors and outdoors
- Divides the space so that infants can play in small groups
- Keeps toys on low, sturdy shelves within reach
- Stores small items in see-through boxes
- Creates interesting obstacle courses for babies who are learning to crawl, cruise, walk, and climb
- Provides a reliable rhythm that meets babies' needs for frequent eating and resting

Changing Area

The changing table should be waist high for adults' comfort and have a washable surface. Changing supplies, a sink with hot and cold running water, and a covered trash container should be in easy reach. Having a nonbreakable mirror behind the changing table is fun for babies.

The changing table needs to be set up with the caregiver in mind. Items should be easy to reach and well organized to minimize the chance of skipping steps in proper diapering and handwashing procedures.

Feeding Areas

The infant room should include places to warm bottles and to sit comfortably while bottle feeding a baby. A quiet corner with a rocking chair is ideal. There should also be a comfortable, private space for nursing mothers.

Babies between 9 and 14 months are also eating solid food and may enjoy having mealtimes at the table, especially if this is what they are used to at home. You can use highchairs, table-height feeding chairs, or seats that attach to a regular table. Make sure the chairs have seatbelts that can restrain a baby who suddenly learns to stand and that they are sturdy enough so that they can't be tipped over by a cruising toddler. In many programs, older babies eat their meals at small tables with sturdy chairs they can climb in and out of.

Bouncy Chairs and Swings (Caution!)

While bouncy chairs and swings give children the opportunity of seeing the world from a sitting position, they need to be selected carefully and used with caution. Bouncy chairs and swings should have safety belts and should not be placed in doorways where they may block emergency access. Confining babies in chairs or swings for too long a period deprives them of opportunities to learn new motor skills, such as rolling over, sitting, and crawling. Walkers with wheels should never be used in an early childhood setting. There is too much of a danger of colliding with another child, rolling over someone's fingers, tipping over, or getting stuck.

Storage Areas for Infant Supplies

Infants come with lots of supplies! You'll need places to store clean diapers, extra clothes, food, and perhaps even car seats for each child.

Play Areas

An infant room should have safe, easily cleaned areas where infants can play together. Low shelves, foam dividers, couches, a play yard or corral, and an empty wading pool can all be used to define intimate spaces and provide support for pulling up and cruising. Mirrors, "busy boxes," and laminated pictures can be mounted at different heights to intrigue babies who are learning to sit, crawl, stand, and walk.

Peep holes, hiding places (visible to an adult), crawling tunnels, large vinyl blocks, low windows, and different colors and textures on the floor help make spaces interesting for babies who are just learning to get around.

Put a sheet on the carpeted play area so that you can wash it daily.

Selecting Learning Materials

Shelf Toys

No infant should be left during a wakeful period without access to age-appropriate toys. Keep some of the toys where babies can get them themselves—on low shelves, in play areas and crawl spaces, or mounted on the walls or on the backs of shelf units.

Here are some toys that are appropriate for babies in the following age groups:

- *3 to 6 months:* rattles, soft squeak toys, cradle gyms, musical toys, washable dolls, animals
- *6 to 9 months:* toy telephones, roly-poly toys, pop-up toys, colorful wheel toys, unbreakable mirrors, washable cuddle toys
- *9 to 14 months:* "busy boards," fill and dump toys, rolling toys, push and pull toys, large balls, soft blocks, cloth or cardboard blocks

Crib Toys

Although the amount of awake time that infants spend in their cribs should be minimized, age-appropriate toys should be placed in every crib:

> *Although the amount of awake time that infants spend in their cribs should be minimized, age-appropriate toys should be placed in every crib.*

- *3 months and under:* crib mobiles that attach to the side of the crib or hang from the ceiling, wind chimes, musical mobiles, see-through crib bumpers
- *4 to 7 months:* cradle gyms, see-through rattles, clutch balls, teething rings
- *8 to 14 months:* "busy boxes," squeak toys, rattles, soft cloth dolls, clutch balls, pop-up toys, and mirror toys

Sensory Bin

Infants enjoy a variety of sensory experiences, such as splashing water, finger painting with pudding, and rubbing their hands in wet cornstarch. A large dishpan is ideal for this kind of play. You can put it and the babies into an empty plastic wading pool to help contain the mess.

Music Area

A cassette recorder, CD player, or record player is a must in an infant play area. "Easy-listening" music, lullabies, nursery rhymes, and classical music provide satisfying listening experiences for infants and their caregivers. You might also encourage parents to record and share the songs or chants that they use with their babies.

Arranging the Infant Room

The way an infant room is arranged depends on how large the room is, how many infants there are, how many staff members are in the room at any one time, the age and mobility of the infants, and whether the room is single purpose (sleeping, eating, or playing) or multipurpose. Looking at the room with a "baby's-eye view," you may see things you want to change as the babies develop new capabilities and interests.

In every situation, however, there are some prime considerations for setting up an infant environment. Arrange the room or rooms according to these guidelines:

- Provide a separation between awake and sleeping babies.
- Make sure that changing tables and feeding areas can be accessed easily from both the sleeping and play areas.
- Provide easy access to running water, refrigeration, covered waste disposal cans, and some type of food warmer.

Looking at the room with a "baby's-eye view," you may see things you want to change as the babies develop new capabilities and interests.

- Designate an adult "lookout spot" with full visibility.
- Carpet the floor of the crib area for quiet and easy clean-up.
- Enclose the play area and make sure that it has a soft but washable surface.
- Arrange toys and books on shelves and group similar items.
- Make sure the CD, cassette, or record player is in easy reach for adults but out of reach of children.
- Allow a 2-foot-wide walkway at all exits. Keep exits clear in accordance with fire safety laws.
- Make sure the arrangement works for the babies and for you.

To set up an environment that takes into account the behavioral characteristics, needs, and interests of young toddlers (14–24 months)

Consider these qualities of young toddlers in setting up a room for them:

- *Young toddlers spend long stretches of time in active play.* Cots can be stacked, except during naptime, and the same room can be used for sleep and play.
- *Young toddlers are developing their large-muscle skills and need opportunities to practice running, climbing, throwing, pushing, pulling, and carrying things around.* The young toddler classroom should provide indoor slides, indoor climbing structures, riding toys, and rocking boats.
- *Young toddler need different kinds of spaces—large, open spaces that let them explore space and small, cozy places that make them feel comfortable and secure.* Create both a large, open space and cozy, crawl-in spaces, such as playhouses, cartons, and corners.
- *Young toddlers are just learning to say "It's mine" and for the most part have not learned about sharing.* They cannot understand why some things, like toys, have to be shared while other things, like lunches and shoes, cannot be shared. Make sure that most of the toys and equipment in the classroom are

conducive to group play. The presence of very attractive one-of-a-kind toys can initiate power struggles.

- *Young toddlers are delighted with rhythm, music, pictures, and books.* Your classroom should have a CD or tape player, a collection of CDs or tapes, attractive pictures at the child's level, and a library corner with indestructible books.

- *Young toddlers tend to be exuberant and excitable and can quickly make a shambles of a classroom.* Simplify the task of cleaning up. Limit the number of small, loose toys that are kept within reach of children. Provide attractive containers for toys that make cleaning up fun. A carton "cage" or Noah's ark can be used as a container for toy animals. A corner of the classroom with lines drawn on the floor or marked on the carpet can be a "parking lot" for wheel toys. Colorful plastic laundry baskets make great storage containers for balls and beanbags.

- *Young toddlers are active and can be very noisy.* With the exception of areas that are used for eating, art, and water play, the room for young toddlers should be carpeted. Also, if possible, there should be acoustic tiles on the ceiling to absorb sound.

- *Young toddlers learn through active exploration.* Provide areas in the classroom where toddlers can finger paint, play with water and clay, experience different textures, and create different sounds. Create a texture wall where the children can feel different surfaces (hard, soft, smooth, rough, furry, slippery, bumpy) or a sound wall where the children can ring a bell, toot a horn, squeak a rubber animal, or beat a drum.

- *Young toddlers are creatures of habit and thus disturbed by too many changes in their environment.* Once you have created an attractive and orderly classroom, change the basic layout as little as possible. Young toddlers gain a sense of security by finding everything in its place. It is especially important for them to have their own special private space (a cubby or a shelf) that is never changed or disturbed.

For more information on the characteristics of young toddlers, see the Developmental Picture.

Equipping a Young Toddler Room

Tables and Chairs

One- to two-year-olds enjoy sitting at tables and chairs, not only for eating but also for sensory experiences, puzzle play, and art activities. Tables should be toddler size (16 to 18 inches high).

Highchairs

By age 1fi, most children can eat comfortably at a low table-and-chair combination. For younger children who are still learning to feed themselves, however, it is best to have highchairs or table-height feeding chairs. By using individualized eating schedules, a room only needs a couple of highchairs, not one for every child.

Developmental Picture

The older infant (9–14 months):

- Is creeping, cruising, and learning to walk and may be practicing walking and climbing skills
- Has favorite toys and is interested in selecting her own toys
- Enjoys emptying and filling containers and holding soft, cuddly things
- Is interested in exploring new spaces
- Can suddenly become overtired and/or overstimulated

The caregiver:

- Provides space and equipment for active movement indoors and out
- Divides the space so that infants can play in small groups
- Keeps toys on low, sturdy shelves within reach
- Stores small items in see-through boxes
- Creates interesting obstacle courses for babies who are learning to crawl, cruise, walk, and climb
- Provides a reliable rhythm that meets babies' needs for frequent eating and resting

The young toddler (14–24 months):

- Is practicing large-muscle skills and may be an active climber
- Enjoys emptying filling, dumping, and pouring
- Enjoys sensory play using materials such as water, rice, sand, and shaving cream
- Likes to play alongside others with matching toys
- Enjoys pretend play
- Is developing a sense of where things belong
- Becomes overstimulated by active activities and is calmed by quiet activities

The caregiver:

- Provides space and equipment for active play both indoors and out, such as push, pull, and scooting toys; slides and climbers; and large, lightweight blocks
- Provides duplicates of favorite items
- Provides simple materials for pretend play, such as purses, scarves, brooms, sponges, telephones, plastic dishes, and cooking pots
- Stores toys on low shelves
- Outdoors, separates the wheeled toy area from the climbing area
- Provides a separate area for eating, with low tables and right-sized chairs
- Maintains a consistent daily rhythm that alternates quiet and active activities and that provides toddlers with a sense of order and time

Arranging the Young Toddler Room

The young toddler room combines some of the features of the infant room with some of the features of the older toddler room. Like infants, young toddlers need a place to sleep, a place to eat, and a place to play, and their caregivers need a place for changing diapers.

Like older toddlers, younger toddlers need larger places for active play; a place for imaginative play; a quiet place for reading a book, playing with manipulatives, and playing alone or with a friend; and a place for sensory play.

Before you can decide where to put the different areas, you first need to look at the "givens" in your room.

- Windows provide light and views but also take up wall space. You may want to put tables for eating and art activities in front of the windows, saving your walls for other activities.

- Doors need to be kept clear as emergency exits. Closet doors that open out create dead spaces in the room when clearances are allowed.

- Carpeted areas are best for active play, circle time activities, and other activities in which children sit on the floor. Tiled areas provide easy clean-up for feeding, sensory play, and art activities.

- The locations of electrical outlets will determine where you put the CD or tape player, bottle warmer, refrigerator, and microwave oven.

- Corners are ideal for quiet play.

- Built-in furnishings will determine the locations of storage spaces. Since you want to limit the number of toys available in the room at the same time, you will need plenty of storage for toys, art materials, and other equipment. Remember to provide storage for your personal belongings, as well as for the children's.

- Use high wall space for the parent information board and for posting emergency plans and phone numbers. Use child-level wall space for sound and texture boards, mirrors, photos of the children and their families, and a flannel-board for displaying the children's creations.

Next, make a rough diagram that indicates the placement of major furnishings and equipment, taking into account all of these fixed features.

Setting Up and Equipping Activity Centers

Your room should include the following basic areas or activity centers.

Greeting Area

The greeting area should include a place where children can store their personal belongings, such as cubbies. Parent boards also are most visible in this area, as are teacher boards.

Eating, Sensory Play, and Creative Art Area

This area will include toddler-sized tables and chairs, highchairs if needed, storage for art and craft supplies, and at least one chair that you can sit on comfortably. Ideally, the eating area should also include a small refrigerator, a microwave oven, running water with disposable paper towels, and a covered garbage can.

Toileting/Diapering Area

Most children under 2 are still in diapers, so you should include a changing table, a diaper bin, and a storage unit for clean diapers and supplies. Access to hot and cold running water is a must. You will also need potty chairs if you do not have access to small toilets for those children who are ready to give up diapers.

Pretend Play Area

Early pretending is very simple and has a strong imitative quality. Children replay experiences that are familiar to them, such as driving, sleeping, cooking, and eating. Having a toddler-sized stove, sink, and table and a doll-sized highchair and crib will encourage early pretending. Make sure, too, that there are places for dishes, cooking utensils, play food, and, of course, ethnically appropriate dolls. Nice additions to the pretend area also include an unbreakable mirror; dress-up jewelry, ties, scarves, purses, and carry-alls; and a "steering wheel" chair to serve as a pretend vehicle.

Active Play Area

Climbing Structures Because young toddlers spend much of their day practicing their motor skills, the choice of climbing structures is critical. The size and number of climbing structures that are placed in the room depends on several factors:

- How much space you have
- How many children are using the space
- How well equipped your playground is
- How much outdoor time the weather permits

Desirable climbing structures include the following:

- *Slides:* A slide is an important piece of basic equipment. A good indoor slide has a crawl space underneath and is designed so that the stairs are easy to mount.
- *Rocking boat:* A rocking boat that converts to a staircase is a particularly desirable structure. It provides opportunities to practice different motor skills and at the same time encourages cooperative play.
- *Special structures:* Ramps, wedges, tunnels, and platforms can provide further practice in motor skills. Again, it is important to remember that young toddlers need room to move around. A desirable climbing structure that takes up too much space is really not desirable.

Blocks   Blocks can be either large cardboard bricks, large nesting blocks, or vinyl-covered shapes.

Push/Ride-On Toys   Young toddlers are also on the move. Cars and trucks that can be ridden, pushed, and pulled will keep them busy.

Music   Every young toddler room should include a cassette tape recorder, CD player, or record player. This should be placed on a relatively high shelf along with the tapes, CDs, or records, and if the equipment is not battery operated, it should be located near an electric outlet. One- to two-years-olds should not have access to this equipment. Rhythm instruments also require a storage bin out of reach of the children so that their use can be controlled.

Quiet Play Areas

Cuddle-Up Structures   Young toddlers need closed, protected, quiet spaces just as much as they need spaces to move around in. Cushions wedged in a corner, foam forms, beanbag chairs, and large cardboard boxes with cut-out "windows" are some ideas for creating private spaces.

Reading Corner   Cuddle-up spaces can also double as reading corners. Place cuddly stuffed animals in the cuddle-up area and a small book display rack within easy reach.

To set up an environment that takes into account the behavioral characteristics, needs, and interests of older toddlers (2 years)

Mr. By-the-Book had just read a book on setting up a toddler environment. He loved the book's suggestions on creating open spaces and interest centers and decided to set up his room exactly like the diagram in the book. When he completed the task, he asked the director to come in and admire it.

The director was at a loss for words. She congratulated him on his hard work and told him the room looked great, but there was one small problem: She didn't see the cots.

Mr. By-the-Book explained that he had put the cots in the empty room across the hall. "I arranged the room exactly like the diagram in the book you lent me," he told her proudly. "I didn't have room for everything, so I decided I would just put the cots down the hall and bring them back for naptime."

"You need to put the cots back in the classroom," the director explained gently. "Unfortunately, our toddler room isn't nearly as large as the one in the book, and you can't simply follow a diagram. Try rearranging the room, leaving space for the cots." ●

As you read about the suggested layout for a toddler room, you will undoubtedly have the same problems as Mr. By-the-Book. If you do not have enough room to follow all of our recommendations, you will have to make compromises. Keep the essential furnishings in the room and work around them. And remember: Not all things have to be available all of the time. Although some basics should remain constant, your room can change over time as the children develop new interests and capabilities.

Characteristics and Interests of Older Toddlers

Older toddlers are about 2 years old and have these characteristics and interests:

- *Older toddlers are practicing emerging motor skills and enjoy running, jumping, twirling, and marching to music.* The classroom needs open spaces where children can engage in active circle time activities.
- *Older toddlers are interested in exploring different kinds of spaces.* The classroom should include a variety of different space experiences, such as a tunnel, a pit, a platform, a bridge, a two-level townhouse, and/or an indoor climbing structure.
- *Older toddlers enjoy quiet, cozy spaces.* The classroom should include a comfortable hideaway spot. It may be a corner with cushions and bolsters, a carton to crawl into, a playhouse, or a hideaway reading corner.
- *Older toddlers are beginning to learn about sharing and turn taking.* The classroom should include some toys for side-by-side play and some toys like blocks and wagons that encourage cooperation.
- *Older toddlers enjoy constructive play.* The classroom should have a carpeted block area, where children have easy access to a variety of plastic and cardboard blocks.
- *Older toddlers are interested in creating with different kinds of materials.* The classroom should have access to fluid and pliable materials, such as water, sand, easel paint, clay, and crayons.
- *Older toddlers are becoming more sophisticated in their pretend play.* The classroom should contain play structures, props, and dress-up material for involved types of pretending and small representational objects, such as toy animals, vehicles, and dolls, for more simple pretending.
- *Older toddlers are experiencing a rapid growth in language skills.* The classroom should be well stocked with culturally and thematically appropriate picture books, tapes, prints, and photos that encourage receptive and expressive language.

See the following Developmental Picture (page 64) for more on the interests and activities of older toddlers.

Developmental Picture

The older toddler (2-year-old):

- Pushes, pulls, and carries things around
- Enjoys practicing motor skills
- Is interested in simple dress-up clothes and pretend play
- Pulls toys off the shelves
- Enjoys choosing books, toys, and puzzles
- Recognizes where things belong

The caregiver:

- Provides an area for imaginative play and an area for motor activities
- Recognizes that children will mix toys from different areas as they combine them in play
- Keeps a variety of toys within easy reach
- Maintains an orderly classroom and a consistent but flexible routine
- Provides ample time for activities and care routines so the atmosphere can be relaxed

Equipping the Room for Older Toddlers

A room for older toddlers should contain the following equipment.

Tables and Chairs

Older toddlers enjoy sitting at tables for snacks, mealtimes, arts and craft activities, and manipulative play. Follow these specifications in choosing tables and chairs:

- *Size:* The tables for older toddlers should be approximately 18 inches high; the chairs should fit under the tables, allowing enough space for leg room.
- *Number:* Because older toddlers enjoy meal- and snacktimes together, it is important to have a chair and room at a table for each child.
- *Shape:* The shape and size of the tables depends on how the classroom is arranged. If the same tables are used for snacktime, art projects, and manipulative activities, it is important to have small tables that can be moved. Rectangular or trapezoidal tables work better than round ones for arts and crafts and can be put together in different configurations and then taken apart.

Structures

Toddlers love to climb and explore, both alone and together. A loft with a ladder serves several purposes. It challenges toddlers to climb up, gives them a bird's-eye view, and provides spaces above and below where two or three friends can have private playtime. At the same time, it presents endless possibilities for pretend play. Add a blanket, and it becomes a tent for going camping or giving a circus performance. Add a steering wheel, and it's a car, a truck, an airplane, a boat, or a rocket ship. Make sure the loft is sturdy enough and the railings high enough to support jumping toddlers.

Shelves and Room Dividers

Because older toddlers enjoy a room that is organized into play centers, it is important to have enough shelving, book racks, and room dividers to section off the classroom.

Selecting Materials and Toys

Pretend Play Props and Equipment

The amounts and types of pretend play equipment depend both on budget constraints and the size of the classroom. A well-equipped older toddler classroom will include six types of pretend play equipment:

1. Equipment for "kitchen" play, including a stove, refrigerator, sink, highchair, mop or broom, and table and chairs

2. Equipment for "store" or puppet play, including a puppet stage that converts into a grocery store, post office, or bank

3. Equipment for doll play, including a variety of ethnic dolls plus a crib, a carriage, blankets, and a box with doll clothes

4. Dress-up play equipment, including a mirror and appropriate storage for costumes, shoes, purses, and jewelry

5. Equipment for "driver" play, such as a shopping cart or doll carriage, a riding toy or steering wheel, chairs that can be lined up to make a train, and a large box or laundry basket the children can climb into and use as a boat, racing car, or jeep

6. An assortment of miniature play sets, such as a farm, zoo, restaurant, dollhouse, garage, train, and fire station, with the accompanying props and miniature characters

To organize and equip a preschool classroom that promotes different kinds of play and learning experiences and that reflects the interests, needs, ability levels, and family backgrounds of the children (3–5 years)

Two preschool teachers from different schools were having dinner together. Miss Free Thinker, who worked in the Creative Workshop Preschool, began the conversation:

Miss Free Thinker: "Boy, am I glad it's Friday. School begins on Monday, and I spent most of the week moving furniture and arranging shelves. I do feel it was worth it, though. I needed to add a pretend play area and a science discovery area. Now, the room looks great."

Miss Discontented: "Well, you know I took a job at the College Prep Preschool, and we never have to change the room arrangement. The teacher sits at the desk in front of the room and the children sit at tables, two children per table, facing the teacher's desk."

Miss Free Thinker: "Do you like that arrangement?"

Miss Discontented: "Personally, I hate it, but it goes along with the philosophy of the school. The director believes that the best way to get children ready for success in school is to teach them academics, and so you should arrange the room like an elementary classroom. It sets the right tone."

Miss Free Thinker: "Do you agree?"

Miss Discontented: "I told you, I hate it, but that's the way the director wants it, and the parents are all right there behind her. So, as long as I stay in the school, I am not going to rock the boat." ●

This book is built on the philosophy that children are active learners who do best in environments that encourage exploration, imagination, and creativity. The suggestions for organizing learning environments provided in this chapter are a reflection of that philosophy.

Characteristics and Interests of Preschool Children

Just as infant and toddler classrooms are designed to meet the special needs of very young children, preschool classrooms must take into account the social, emotional, and intellectual characteristics of 3-, 4-, and 5-year-olds and the cultural backgrounds of these children. Consider the following:

- *The preschool child appreciates a beautiful classroom.* The preschool classroom should be inviting and attractive. If there is a choice, the walls should be painted a neutral or light pastel color, and pictures and materials should be added to provide the color. Shelves are critical. Even the best-equipped classrooms are often short of shelf space. Shelves serve the double function of dividing space into discrete areas and providing a place where toys and learning materials are accessible to children.
- *The preschool child enjoys an orderly classroom.* Materials should be arranged and coded so that everything in the classroom has its appropriate place. An ideal plan is to color code or picture code the shelves and materials so that it is easy to remember where everything belongs.
- *The preschool child needs a variety of social experiences with large-group, small-group, and individual activities.* The classroom should provide a variety of spaces for each, which may include the following:
  - *Large-group space:* A circle on the carpet, individual mats that can be placed in a circle on a carpet, and round or trapezoid tables all facilitate large-group interaction.
  - *Small-group space:* Interesting areas where the space is defined by lofts or corner enclosures encourage children to interact in small groups.
  - *Individual space:* Private, "all-by-myself" time can be provided by a reading corner with large pillows or beanbag chairs, a telephone booth structure, or even a large carton with a fuzzy rug on the bottom.

- *The preschool child likes to feel at home.* Make the children feel that the classroom is an extension of their home and a part of their neighborhood by providing a careful selection of family photos on the walls, materials such as play foods that are familiar to them, dress-up clothes that resemble the clothes the adults they know are likely to wear, dolls that look like the children in the classroom, and rhythm instruments that are used in the ceremonies they attend.

- *Preschool children need help to learn to be considerate of each other.* A classroom should be arranged to make it easy for children to be considerate. Noisy areas for music, block play, and pretend play should be separated from quiet areas, such as the library corner or problem-solving areas. Shelves should be used to control the traffic flow so that children won't upset each other's work.

- *Preschool children are ready to make activity selections.* Whether a preschool classroom is large or small, it should be organized into learning or interest centers. Both the number and the types of interest centers depend on the size and configuration of the classroom, the objectives of the curriculum, the staffing pattern, and the ages and characteristics of the children.

- *Preschool children enjoy working at tables.* Tables and chairs should be placed in the art and snack area and in some of the work areas. Children may enjoy using tables for practicing writing, putting puzzles together, setting up scenes with miniature figures, and playing math or language games.

- *The preschool child needs opportunities to pretend.* Every preschool classroom should provide spaces and equipment for imaginative play. Housekeeping equipment, a dress-up corner, a mirror, a telephone, dolls, and dishes are basic requirements. Other items can be added to reflect the children's interests, home cultures, and favorite stories as well as the themes that the teacher has introduced.

- *The preschool child must have experience with music and art.* The classroom should be equipped with a CD, tape, or record player; a variety of music, including marches, folk songs, and nursery rhymes; simple musical instruments; and a place where children can sit or march in a circle. For art, there should be tables and chairs, a sink, a noncarpeted floor area, and plenty of eye-level wall space where the children's work can be attractively displayed. Easels, drying racks, and whiteboards are desirable, as well.

- *Preschool children need opportunities to play with blocks and to work with a variety of construction toys.* Every preschool classroom should have a block area where children can learn to construct. Block play helps children develop their imagination and creativity and, at the same time, teaches mathematical and spatial concepts. Providing miniature figures, toy animals, cars and trucks, and small balls encourages children to build pretend worlds and raceways.

- *Preschool children are developing their language and communication skills.* A preschool classroom should provide spaces and materials that encourage language development. Picture books, display counters, eye-level wall treatments, puppet stages, elevated platforms, mirrors, cameras, and tape recorders can all be used to encourage language development.

- *Preschool children are ready and eager to learn new concepts.* A preschool classroom should include spaces and materials for manipulative play, problem solving, and science exploration. The traditional preschool science and discovery corner should not be simply a display area; rather, it should provide opportunities for hands-on experiences, including the following:

  —*Science and discovery:* pets (check with the local health department), plants, sink-and-float activities, magnet challenges, shells and rocks that can be classified, a scale, prisms, magnifying glasses, color paddles, and a sand table

  —*Manipulative play and problem solving:* a variety of materials that encourage sorting, ordering, number skill development, and pattern making, such as number puzzles, pegboards, table blocks, picture puzzles, counting games, stacking toys, color and shape games, sequencing boards, beads, and sewing cards

The Development Picture below provides additional information about the interests and abilities of preschoolers.

Arranging the Preschool Classroom

In order to meet the specific needs of the preschool child, it is important to take a broad look at the way the space is utilized—that is, to see the "big picture." To begin, we need to consider three factors:

Developmental Picture

The preschool child (3–5 years):

- Is an active learner
- Is developing a sense of self
- Is learning to play with others
- Can put toys away in the right places
- Recognizes and can choose a special interest area
- Learns through playing with dramatic play materials, blocks, manipulatives, art materials, and books
- Is likely to want some choices about what to do and when

The caregiver:

- Provides a rich variety of experiences and materials
- Defines activity areas, such as pretend play, science/discovery, art, language, blocks, and manipulative play
- Encourages choices
- Provides symbols or color codes to help children put toys away in the appropriate places
- Provides a daily routine that balances active/quiet, individual/group, and indoor/outdoor activities

- How can we use space to control group size?
- How can we separate noisy and quiet spaces?
- How can we control traffic flow?

Using Space to Control Group Size

We have said that children need opportunities to spend time in large groups, in small groups, and by themselves. A carefully engineered classroom provides areas that invite different-sized groups. A circle in the middle of the floor is an invitation to form a large group. A table for two or three, an interest area set off by bookshelves, a loft, or a playhouse invites children to cluster in small groups. "All-by-myself" places can be created in a book corner with a rocking chair, a small carton "house," and a beanbag chair that faces the wall.

Separating Noisy and Quiet Areas

In a well-designed classroom, there is a separation of noisy and quiet activities. Activities that require concentration, such as reading, problem solving, and practicing language skills, are on one side of the classroom. Noisy activities, like block building, climbing, and music, are on the other side. Art and imaginative play, which are relatively quiet activities that do not require excessive concentration, can be done in areas that serve as buffers.

Controlling Traffic Flow

The placement of furniture can be used to discourage Follow-the-Leader games and to encourage the formation of small groups. The placement of furniture also can be used to discourage children from interfering with each other. A block area that is arranged as an interest area, with only one space for exiting and entering, provides a safe place to build a structure.

Other Factors to Consider

Other factors should also be considered in arranging a successful space for 3- to 5-year-olds:

- What kind of floor covering to use
- What kinds of work and play surfaces work best
- How to make the best use of wall space
- How to create interest centers

Floor Covering

Floor covering is an important consideration in designing a preschool setting. A low-pile carpet is great for most of the classroom, but a vinyl-type floor covering is best for the "messy activity" areas. The sink area, snack area, art corner, and science and discovery area should be set over vinyl or similar floor covering to allow for quick, easy clean-up. Smaller pieces of carpet can be used to define specific playing areas, where a child can take an activity and be on his own private "island." Alternatively, if the entire floor is carpeted, vinyl remnants can be placed in messy areas.

Work and Play Surfaces

Thought should be given to providing open-space areas (versus tables) near display units. Some activities work better at tables than on the floor and vice versa. Table work is often approached more seriously by children and should be encouraged with activities requiring concentration and problem solving.

To direct traffic to a table or floor space, simply place a table close to shelves displaying table work activities and leave open floor space near other activities. Don't be too concerned about separating table from floor activities. Children will often make this distinction according to their own set of rules. Keep in mind that a good use of space allows 35 square feet (about the size of a king-sized bed) of unencumbered space per child.

Wall Space

In most classrooms, wall space is at a premium. Walls are taken up by sinks, doors, windows, shelves, and storage units. This means that all available display wall space has to be used wisely.

Here are some suggestions:

- Make sure that you have posted all items required by the licensing bureau, which are likely to include the following:
  — A fire escape plan
  — Emergency telephone numbers
  — A daily schedule
- A high priority in using wall space is to display children's products. Make sure that the products are hung at the child's eye level in an attractive arrangement.
- Use some accessible walls for conversation starters. These can be posters, photographs taken on field trips, interesting things that children have said, and displays relating to what the children are investigating.
- If your classroom is divided into interest centers, tie in the wall decoration with the purpose of an interest center. The housekeeping wall could have a mock window with an outdoor scene, or when it changes to a "doctor's office" or "veterinary hospital," post a sign saying "The doctor is in."
- Display photos of children and their families in places where children can point to and talk about them.
- Put up words. Put children's names on their cubbies, family photos, and artwork. Label each interest center with its current theme. Post appropriate reminders, such as "Close door gently."

Setting Up Interest Centers

An *interest center* is a defined classroom area that can accommodate three to six children. Some interest centers, like a block area or an art table, remain the same throughout the year. Others, like a "firehouse," puppet stage, or "science museum" may change with the curriculum units and the children's interests. Some areas, such as a wood-working center or cooking center, may be open only when you have extra help.

The following sections describe some interest centers that work well in most preschool classrooms. You, the children, and their families will certainly add others.

Imaginative Play Center

Type of Space Semienclosed. Carpeted. Child-sized furniture. Shelving for play materials. A mirror and clothes storage. A loft or other play structure adds space and flexibility.

Pretend Play Area

Type of Play	Benefits	Equipment and Materials
Doll play	• Consolidates experiences • Encourages care and empathy	Multicultural dolls, doll bed, stroller, highchair, blankets, clothes, bathing tub, diaper set, feeding items like bottles, bibs
Kitchen play	• Encourages cooperative play • Provides practice in playing a grown-up role • Encourages helping behavior	Telephone, stove, sink, refrigerator, small table and chairs, dishes, tableware, pots and pans, tablecloth, placemats, pot holders, oven mitt, baking utensils, toaster
Cleaning and housekeeping	• Encourages helping behavior • Provides practice in playing a grown-up role • Develops new skills	Brooms, mops, dustpans, carpet sweepers, scrub brushes, feather dusters
"Store"	• Creates a feeling of power • Invites cooperative play • Develops number skills	Cash register, balance scale, paper bags, play money, stamps, empty cans, boxes, play food
"Doctor/Nurse"	• Helps children cope with fears • Gives children a feeling of power • Encourages cooperation	Play stethoscope and thermometer, Band-Aids, gauze and tape, sling, diploma, eye chart, blood pressure cuff, flashlight, doctor and nurse uniforms, empty medicine bottles, spoons, prescription pad, play syringe

Dress-Up Play Area

Type of Play	Benefits	Equipment and Materials
Dress-up	• Provides practice in role-playing • Encourages creativity • Builds self-confidence • Provides practice in dressing and undressing	Firefighter and police hats, masks, mirrors, purses, wallets, keys, "credit cards," suitcases, clothing racks Clothing: shirts, dresses, capes, vests, shawls, scarves, robes, ties, belts Footwear: slippers, boots, shoes

Constructive Play Area

Type of Play	Benefits	Equipment and Materials
Constructive	• Encourages creativity • Promotes cooperation • Develops numerical concepts • Improves small-muscle development • Promotes language	Blocks of various types and sizes: unit blocks, large plastic interlocking or stacking blocks, small fit-together blocks like large Legos, bristle blocks, giant dominos Accessories such as vehicles, people, zoo and farm animals

Move-and-Grow Center

Type of Space Large and open; relatively noisy. Carpeted. Storage space for large equipment and rhythm instruments. CD, tape, or record player.

Movement Area

Type of Play	Benefits	Equipment and Materials
Large muscle	• Develops large-muscle skills • Provides an outlet for energy • Provides opportunities for group play	Tumbling mat, walking board, balance beam, Hop Scotch or number line, skipping rope, beanbags, large sit-on trucks, train

A carefully engineered classroom provides areas that invite different-sized groups.

Music Area

Type of Play	Benefits	Equipment and Materials
Music	• Develops an appreciation of music • Improves coordination and rhythm • Develops listening skills • Provides opportunities for self-expression	Rhythm instruments; CD, tape, or record player; CDs, tapes, or records; scarves, songbooks

Create and Discover Center

Type of Space Large and noisy. Uncarpeted. Sink, tables and chairs, shelves for craft materials, table for science and discovery displays, sand and water tables, hot plate.

Science and Discovery Area

Type of Play	Benefits	Equipment and Materials
Sorting and classifying	• Develops observation and discrimination skills	Rocks, shells, beans, nuts, seeds, small containers, magnifying glass, mystery boxes, labels
Encouraging investigation	• Helps children use their senses for investigation	Water table with sieves, basters, funnels, pitchers, bottles, measuring cups, egg beaters
Manipulation	• Provides opportunities for sensory play and investigation	Sand table with sifter, different-shaped containers, scoops, shovels, spoons
Discovery	• Develops problem solving	Magnets and metal objects, sink-and-float tub, lab book
Sharpening of senses	• Develops observation and use of senses	Kaleidoscope, color paddles, sound-and-smell containers, prisms
Growth center	• Develops observation and nurturance	Pots, seeds, shovels, ruler, graph paper
Pet center	• Develops nurturance and responsibility	Goldfish, hamster, ant farm, guinea pig, pet care books, notebook

The traditional preschool science and discovery corner should not be simply a display area but should provide opportunities for hands-on experiences.

Cooking Area

Type of Play	Benefits	Equipment and Materials
Cooking	<ul><li>Provides opportunities to use all the senses</li><li>Helps children to learn about food and nutrition</li><li>Develops small-muscle coordination</li><li>Stimulates language and concept</li><li>Helps children learn to follow directions</li></ul>	Heat source: stove, hotplate, or electric pan Refrigerator and sink (ideal but not essential) Other kitchen equipment: table and chairs, pots and pans, cooking utensils, recipe board, chef hats and smocks, cleaning materials, food and recipes, large paper for displaying recipes

Arts and Crafts Area

Type of Play	Benefits	Equipment and Materials
Painting	<ul><li>Encourages expression</li></ul>	Easels, brushes, paper, rollers, paints, drying rack or clothes line
Crafts	<ul><li>Develops artistic sense</li><li>Develops a sense of personal accomplishment</li><li>Encourages exploration in a variety of media</li></ul>	Clay, scissors, scrap materials, paste, tape, wallpaper, books, markers, crayons, colored tissues, cookie cutters, chenille stems, stamps and inkpads, sponges, screen, toothbrushes, hole punches, craft sticks
Weaving	<ul><li>Encourages exploration with materials</li></ul>	Weaving loom, yarn
Collage	<ul><li>Encourages exploration with materials</li></ul>	Cloth and carpet samples, wallpaper, books, ribbons, scraps of paper, buttons and beads, feathers, old magazines and catalogs, recycled items (berry baskets, meat trays, egg cartons, boxes, paper towel rolls)
Wood working	<ul><li>Provides experiences with unusual materials and tools</li></ul>	Scrap pieces of soft wood, safety glasses, wood glue, hammer and nails, vise, sandpaper, paints, patterns and diagrams

Circle Activity Area

Type of Play	Benefits	Equipment and Materials
Circle activity	<ul><li>Provides a place for daily opening and closing activities</li><li>Develops language and listening</li><li>Provides opportunities for participating in large-group activities</li></ul>	Carpet squares for the children to define individual spaces, flannelboard for language activities, chartpaper for recording experience stories

Play and Learn Center

Type of Space Relatively quiet. Carpeted. Shelving for materials, small table and chairs. Computer (optional).

Reading and Writing Readiness

Type of Play	Benefits	Equipment and Materials
Visual skills	• Develops visual skills related to reading	Inset puzzles, beads to string, blocks and pattern-matching cards, picture dominos, Lotto games, block design sets, sequence puzzles
Auditory skills	• Develops listening skills related to reading	Rhyming cards and letter/sound games
Learning the alphabet	• Encourages working alone and completing a task	Tactile letter board, alphabet puzzles, alphabet cards, magnetic letter board
Writing readiness	• Practices motor skills for writing • Develops concepts of print and symbol correspondence • Learns to use simple computer programs	Writing utensils, templates, stencils, chalk and chalkboards, pencils, paper and crayons Wooden tool sets, sewing cards, lacing shoes, geo-form boards, dressing frames, lock boxes Computers with word-processing and picture-making software
Reading	• Develops an appreciation for stories and pictures	A collection of different books from an appropriate bibliography, including "big books," multicultural, teacher-made and child-made books, cassette tapes or CDs with read-along books A quiet corner with comfortable pillows, child-sized couches or easy chairs, camera and film, pictures, posters, puppets

Language and Concept Development

Type of Play	Benefits	Equipment and Materials
Vocabulary development	• Increases vocabulary • Learns classification skills	Picture cards, occupation match-up cards, Lotto games, classification games, category cards, touch-and-match sets, feel tablets, color boards, color tablets, computer stories, storytelling software

(continued)

Type of Play	Benefits	Equipment and Materials
Pattern relationships	• Learns about patterns and relationships	Spatial relationship cards, play tile sets, parquetry blocks, pegboards
Problem-solving skills	• Develops problem-solving skills	"What's missing" games, puzzles, attribute blocks, computer-based treasure hunts

Number Readiness

Type of Play	Benefits	Equipment and Materials
Counting	• Develops concepts of number and sets that prepare the child for learning	Cubes, buttons, counting frame, abacus, bead-o-graph, color and object sorting materials, Montessori beads, computer and board games
Learning sets and numbers	• Helps children make discriminations on the basis of shape, weight, and size	Number cards, peg numbers, Unifix cubes, magnetic numerals and boards, dominos
Learning about shape and size	• Introduces the basic numerical concepts of measurement and quantity	Geometric shapes, fit-a-shape sets, nesting toys, stacking squares, Montessori cylinders, pink tower, long stair, broad stair
Learning about measurement, time, and money	• Introduces tools for measuring size, weight, and time • Provides experiences with money	Balance scale, play money, see-through clock, yardstick, rulers, tape measure, nesting measuring cups

Use low furniture to define areas.

Interest Center Dividers

Use low furniture to define areas. Make sure that the furniture is sturdy. In some areas, it is useful to have double-sided bookcases, which will be accessible to interest areas on both sides.

Other Essentials

For Health and Safety

- A place for toothbrushes and drinking cups
- A fire extinguisher
- A place to post the fire evacuation plan
- A place to keep health records and emergency numbers
- A place for tissues and paper towels
- Wastepaper baskets
- An out-of-reach place for cleaning products
- A locked cabinet for medication

For Personal Possessions

- A special cubby for each child
- A place for you to keep plans, records, and personal items
- A place for cots, mats, and blankets
- A drinking fountain at the children's height or a water bottle for each child
- Some private hideaways or soft spaces where children can be alone

From the Drawing Board to the Classroom

Whether you are arranging a classroom for the first time or simply rearranging an existing classroom, begin your task with a paper and pencil. (It is much easier to erase a line than to move a shelf.) Do these things:

- Draw the outline of your room, putting in doors, windows, fixed furniture and partitions, electrical outlets, sinks, closets, and the like.
- Using circles, lay out your classroom areas, remembering to do the following:
  - Put the art area on a noncarpeted floor near the sink.
  - Put the music center or any interest center requiring electrical power near an electrical outlet.
  - Separate quiet and noisy areas.
- Walk through your classroom with your fingers. Are there any problems with traffic flow?
- Make an inventory of the materials to go in each interest area. Is the area the right size? Is the needed storage available?
- Finally, put down the paper and actually move the furniture and equipment. Make changes and adjustments until things work well.

To organize and equip a learning environment for a multiage or family child care setting that includes children ages birth through 5

Spring had sprung at Growing Together Family Day Care, and the children couldn't wait to get outside. "Here's your coat, Jomo," said 4-year-old Luis to his 2-year-old friend. "Let me help you put it on."

Outside on the playground, Luis and Jomo turned over rocks together, looking for bugs and sprouts. Luis drew an "L" in the damp earth and then showed Jomo how to make a "J." "That gives me an idea," said their teacher. "Let's go to the sandbox and draw shapes and write messages." ●

Today, many parents are choosing family child care because they like its homelike atmosphere. They like the idea that brothers and sisters can be together and that their children will have playmates of different ages. Many centers are also experimenting with *multiage grouping*. They put infants, toddlers, and even preschoolers together,

> *Today, many parents are choosing family child care because they like its homelike atmosphere.*

as they would be in a family, so that the younger children can learn from the older ones and the older children can experience the joy of helping to take care of the younger ones.

Multiage grouping presents the teacher with unique challenges, however. How can she set up a room to accommodate such a range of developmental needs? How can she structure the environment to get the most benefit from multiage grouping?

One way to begin planning for a multiage environment is to block out some key areas:

- A gathering place for the whole group
- A cubby or personal storage space for each child
- Sleeping spaces
- Protected floor space for babies and young toddlers, with sturdy furniture for cruising and climbing
- An active play area for older toddlers and preschoolers
- Some places in lofts and on tables where older children can draw, build, display collections, and work with puzzles and games without interference from the babies
- Spaces for cooking, eating, music, pretending, reading, and looking after pets that everyone can share

Also add some special spaces where children can be alone or spend time with one or two friends—a cardboard box "house," a quiet corner with a beanbag chair or soft pillows, a rocking boat, or a loft. Don't forget about the adults' needs: a rocking chair, places for planning and record keeping, comfortable seating, and safe and efficient setups for diaper changing, food preparation, and (in a home) daily chores and maintenance.

Next, make sure that each area is furnished appropriately, with safe toys that the children can reach. Young babies like to watch older children, so make sure you have an easy way of moving them from place to place, and keep some of their toys within reach. Toddlers like to imitate, so make sure there are items they can use for "cooking," building, reading, art, active sports, and other activities that the older children will be involved in.

Stock up on items with broad age appeal, such as balls, soap bubbles, rubber animals, sensory play and art materials, dolls, and riding toys such as wagons that children of different ages can use together. Store some of the toys in bins, baskets, and other containers so that you can rotate them easily to maintain children's interest. Keep popular toys where children can get at them and put them away easily. You might set up appealing storage spaces, such as a "garage" for cars and trucks under a small table, a basket for balls or beanbags, or a doll "house" on a shelf for miniature figures.

Finally, assess each room or area from different heights. What interesting things can a baby see from an infant seat or from the floor? Where can a crawler go, and what can she get to play with? Where can a young toddler pull up to a stand? What is within his reach? What will stimulate conversations among the older children and encourage them to play together? Will the younger children be able to participate in the older children's games and activities? Is the area safe for all of the children who will use it?

To develop a well-balanced daily schedule

With more parents in the workforce, children's time has become more scheduled. For many children, weekdays involve getting up early, going to one or more child care placements, and returning home late in the day. Most child care centers and family child care homes now operate 10 to 13 hours a day; some have evening and/or weekend hours, as well.

When children are spending significant portions of their waking hours in a child care facility, it is important to establish a daily routine that meets their developmental needs. Although activities will change from day to day, there needs to be a basic schedule that is flexible but predictable.

Planning the Infant's Day

Mrs. Davis was looking for a child care center for her 6-month-old baby. She found the Wee Care Center in the telephone book and made an appointment to visit.

Mrs. Carer (the child care provider): "Oh, yes. We have a fine staff here. We feed our babies on demand and keep them dry and clean at all times."

Mrs. Davis: "That sounds like just what I'm looking for. What sorts of activities do you have for the babies when they are awake?"

Mrs. Carer: "Activities? I told you already that we feed our babies on demand and keep them clean and dry at all times. Oh, I know you might have read about infant curriculums in some of those fancy books, but you can bet your bottom dollar that the people who wrote those books never changed a baby's diaper! If you want to run a real good nursery, you sure don't have time for fun and games!"

Mrs. Carer has obviously not been reading the "fancy books" she complains about, nor has she kept up with the research on infants' brain development. If she has no time for "fun and games," she may be caring for too many babies. In any case, she needs to rethink her schedule so that she has time to talk and play with each baby and engage all the babies in simple activities. Much of the "fun and games," of course, will take place during routine care. As she changes diapers, gets babies up from their naps, feeds and soothes them, and puts them to sleep, Mrs. Carer can take the time to talk with the babies, tickle their tummies, play simple body awareness games, help them pull up into a sitting or standing position, point out interesting sights, and sing songs.

Setting up a simple, basic schedule and spending some time planning for each day could help Mrs. Carer make the time she needs for other activities.

Some Hints on Planning the Day for Infants

Routine and Flexibility Within a child care setting, as at home, it is important to let young infants follow their own feeding and sleeping schedules. At the same time, babies will be more playful and less fussy when their schedules are somewhat predictable. Dividing the day into segments that follow a consistent pattern helps young infants to develop more regular eating and sleeping patterns. Older infants will tend to be more flexible and can begin to adjust to a common eating and sleeping schedule. Infants should be assigned to a specific caregiver so they can establish a relationship with one significant person who knows their schedule and can read their cues.

> *Infants should be assigned to a specific caregiver so they can establish a relationship with one significant person who can read their cues.*

Indoors and Out Infants enjoy spending time each day outside, as long as the weather permits. Riding toys, pull and push toys that need space, and small climbing structures are appropriate for the 12- to 18-month group. Infants who are not walking can be placed outdoors on quilts along with their toys. A patio area covered with tile or indoor/outdoor carpet provides a nice play area. Messy sensory experiences—such as playing with water, soap bubbles, or wet cornstarch—can be conducted outside to minimize clean up.

Quiet and Active Balance quiet times (playing soothing music, rocking, or reading) with more active periods.

Special Times Set aside a special time every day for a sensory activity.

Movement/Music Time Have a regularly planned time so that infants are exposed to music each day.

Books and Language Activities Set aside a quiet time for looking at books and doing language activities to ensure this important area is not neglected.

For more information on planning the day for infants, see the schedule on the following page.

Planning the Day for Toddlers

Young toddlers are very busy trying out new motor and language skills. Given this, they need a lot of watching as they learn to walk, run, and climb and a lot of individual attention as they try to make their wants and discoveries understood with grunts, gestures, and newly learned words. Participation in group activities, such as circle time, is likely to be sporadic and brief. Still, a regular schedule, with a good deal of repetition of favorite activities, provides a comforting rhythm to the day. Rituals like singing "hello" and "good-bye" songs help young toddlers mark time and place and provide a sense of security.

A Basic Schedule for Infants

Arrival Time
Caregivers exchange information with parents and help each baby get comfortable.

Midmorning Playtime (on floor)
Sensory activities, reading, singing, and music/movement. Playing with toys and with caregiver.

Outdoor Time
Outdoor play and sensory activities.

Lunch
For infants who are on solid food; individualized feedings for young infants.

Naptime
For older infants; individualized sleeping for young infants.

Midafternoon Playtime (on floor)
Sensory activities, reading, singing, and music/movement. Playing with toys and with caregiver.

Afternoon Walk
Or time outdoors.

Late Afternoon
Start to organize each infant's belongings for the trip home. Complete the daily report.

Departure
Parents arrive to pick up the infants. Time for communication between caregivers and parents.

Older toddlers also do best with a predictable schedule, and they enjoy learning routines. Rituals at the beginning and end of the day help them feel secure and in control. A comfortable, predictable balance of active and quiet activities helps keep their natural energy and exuberance within bounds. With their short attention span and insatiable curiosity, 2-year-olds tend to flit from one activity to another. At the same time, they may resist transitions that they do not initiate. You can play music or sing special songs to help the children know when it is time to join the circle, clean up, eat, take a nap, or get ready to say good-bye.

A regular schedule, with a lot of repetition of favorite activities, provides a comforting rhythm to the day.

Most toddlers will be able to follow a common schedule when it comes to eating and naptimes (see the box on page 82). But they will still be on their own schedules when it comes to getting drinks of water, diaper changing, and, for some, learning to use the toilet.

A Basic Schedule for Toddlers

Arrival Time
Caregivers exchange information with parents and help each toddler get comfortable.

"Hello" Song
Short circle time (for children who are interested).

Morning Snack or Breakfast

Midmorning Playtime
Music and movement experiences, reading to individual or small groups of children, playing in activity centers; special planned activity for small group.

Outdoor Time

Lunch

Naptime

Midafternoon Playtime
Music and movement experiences, reading to individual or small groups of children, playing in activity centers.

Outdoor Time

Late Afternoon
Start to organize the children's belongings for the trip home. Complete the daily report.

Departure
Parents arrive to pick up the children. Time for communication between caregivers and parents.

Developing a Daily Schedule for Preschoolers

Mrs. Curtis came to visit a child care center. The director brought her to a classroom and invited her to go in and spend some time. She found the teacher, Mrs. Owens, sitting with a small group of children reading a rainbow story. In the center of the room, four children were sitting in a rocking boat singing "Row, Row, Row Your Boat." Several children were trying on old clothes at the far end of the room. In another corner, a boy was working alone building a giant block tower. When Mrs. Owens spotted the visitor, she finished the rainbow story and suggested that the children go to the drawing table and color their own rainbows. When the children she had been reading to got settled making drawings, Mrs. Owens welcomed her guest to the classroom.

Mrs. Curtis looked amazed. "How do you ever do it?" she asked. "You have twelve children in this classroom, and every child seems busy and happy. I've got three kids at home and my house is always in a state of turmoil."

"I've been at it for some time," Mrs. Owens replied modestly.

Although Mrs. Owens made light of her accomplishment, keeping a room of 3-year-olds productively involved in a variety of tasks is not easy. It requires a teacher who is confident, well organized, and adept at engineering a classroom. Let us look at some of the ingredients of good classroom management:

- Developing a daily schedule
- Implementing a daily schedule
- Planning for a "rainy day"
- Transition time

Whether you are a family child care provider taking care of four children or a child care center teacher with a class of twelve, the place to begin good management is with a daily schedule. A schedule is not a curriculum or a daily plan. It does not describe the crafts, lessons, or activities that have been scheduled for the day. It does, however, describe the timetable that you follow on a daily basis throughout the year.

Criteria for Developing an Effective Daily Schedule

A daily schedule must take into account the philosophy of the program, the ages of the children you are working with, the size of the group, the length of the day, the children's patterns of arrival and departure, and the physical setup of the child care facility.

Philosophy

A daily schedule is a reflection of the philosophy of the center. A program that stresses academics will set aside large blocks of time for structured lessons and for play-based activities that promote academic skills. A program that stresses the development of creativity in art, music, and movement will provide time slots in the daily schedule for these activities. A program with a religious orientation may block out time for prayer or religious teaching. A program with a major focus on physical health and nutrition may provide blocks of time for health checks, personal care, and the preparation and serving of nutritious snacks.

Ages of the Children

All preschool children, whether they are 3 years old or 5 years old, are still developing their ideas about time. Most cannot yet read a clock or even understand what is meant by the words *minutes* and *hours*. The best way for children to understand time is through routine events. Events that mark off the day include mealtime, snacktime, circle or whole-group meeting time, playground time, and naptime. Because children perceive time as passing at a much slower rate than adults do, for them a day is very long. Time markers help them to realize that a day goes by in an orderly way and that going-home time will come and can be counted on. The younger the children, the more important it is to have distinct and predictable time markers.

A second way in which a daily schedule takes into account the ages of the children is in the amount of time devoted to group activities. Very young children have a short attention span and cannot be expected to participate in a group experience for more than 10 or 15 minutes.

Length of the Day

A schedule for a full or extended program is necessarily quite different from one for a half-day program. For a short period of time, children and adults enjoy a fast-paced program, in which there are quick changes in activities and little time is spent in making transitions. For a full-day program, it is better to increase the duration of activities and take more time moving from one activity to the next. It is also critically important to provide a balanced day, alternating quiet activities with activities that are faced paced and active.

The two boxes below provide examples of preschool schedules.

A Basic Half-Day Schedule for Preschoolers

8:30 A.M.	Arrival, circle time
8:45 A.M.	Learning centers with small-group activities offered
10:00 A.M.	Snack with conversation
10:15 A.M.	Outdoor play
10:45 A.M.	Learning centers with small-group activities offered
11:30 A.M.	Clean-up
11:40 A.M.	Storytime, songs and games
11:55 A.M.	Prepare for departure

A Basic Full-Day Schedule for Preschoolers

Morning

7:30–9:00 A.M.	Arrival time; Learning centers; breakfast
9:00–9:15 A.M.	Circle time
9:15–10:30 A.M.	Learning centers with small-group activities offered
10:30–11:15 A.M.	Outdoor activities
11:15 A.M.	Wash up; storytime
11:45 A.M.	Lunch; wash up

Afternoon

12:30 P.M.	Look at books; get ready for resting/naps
2:30 P.M.	Snack; put nap items away
2:45 P.M.	Learning centers with small-group activities offered
3:30 P.M.	Outdoor time
4:15 P.M.	Wash up; storytime
4:30 P.M.	Learning centers; children are departing
6:30 P.M.	Closing

Implementing the Daily Schedule

Having a workable schedule posted on the wall is a good first step—but it is only that. By far, the greater challenge is making the schedule work. Here are some guidelines:

- Make sure to differentiate between setting up a *daily schedule* and developing a *daily plan*. A daily plan describes the curriculum to be implemented during the time slots indicated on the schedule.
- Make your daily plans at least a week in advance, so that you can make phone calls, purchase supplies, and prepare materials as needed.
- Read the plan for the next day before you leave the center, and make sure you have all the materials you need.
- Early in the day, build in time for talking with the children about what they are going to do; toward the end of the day, make time to go over with the children what they have done and to talk about plans for the next day. This can be done in small groups or individually.

Planning for a "Rainy Day"

No matter how carefully we plan and how well we have thought out our curriculum, there are always days when our greatest plans must be canceled or our favorite ideas must be scrapped. It rains for the picnic, or there is a three-alarm fire the day the firefighter is supposed to come to class. The bus for the field trip is late, lunch is taking longer to cook than usual, or the visitor you invited is stuck in traffic, and you find yourself with extra time on your hands and a group of restless children. Whatever the problem, it happens to all of us, and so we should be prepared.

The best quick-fix solution for an unexpected waiting time is to have a repertoire of familiar songs with appropriate variations.

Activities for a "Rainy Day"

While a song or finger play is appropriate for filling up a five-minute waiting space, there will inevitably be emergency situations with longer time slots to fill up. The best way to prepare for a "rainy day" is to have an emergency daily plan, with all the appropriate materials put away on the top shelf. These "surprise boxes" can turn a disappointing day into a special one.

Unbirthday Party

Materials: old greeting cards, stickers, glitter, old party hats, tissue paper or foil and ribbons (children can wrap toys from the classroom for the presents), birthday candles (can be stuck in clay, cheese, or Jell-O as well as real cakes or cupcakes).

(continued)

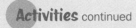 **Activities** continued

Procedure: Let the children help prepare an unbirthday party for the class. Sing "Happy Unbirthday."

Let's Go to the Beach

Materials: shells, pebbles, driftwood, picnic cloth or blanket, story books about sea animals, pails, shovels, and sand molds, "picnic basket" or "cooler."

Procedure: The children can set up a beach scene or make a sandcastle at the sand table, make sandcastles from play dough and decorate them with shells, draw or paint beach scenes and glue on real sand and shells, pack the cooler with pretend food, spread out the blanket, and listen to a beach story. For a change, you can serve lunch or a snack on the picnic blanket instead of at the table.

Edible Art

Materials: recipes and ingredients for chocolate syrup drawing or finger painting (on wax paper), alphabet pretzels, or edible faces (children can make these by decorating paper plates or buttered rice cakes with bits of fruit and vegetables, pieces of cereal, or small crackers).

Procedure: You don't have to save this activity for a "rainy day."

Old Favorites

Materials: toys, books, puzzles, and games that the children have seemed to be finished with.

Procedure: Children will enjoy rediscovering their old toys and will know just what to do with them.

Valentines

Materials: heart cutouts, doilies, stickers, rubber stamps, envelopes, glitter, gold and silver pens, mailbox.

Procedure: Any day can be Valentine's Day.

Train Ride

Materials: train book, engineer's cap, whistle, pictures of exotic places.

Procedure: Put on the cap, line up the chairs, blow the whistle, and call "All aboard." Sing some train songs. Let the children take turns suggesting places to go. Make some suggestions yourself. You might go to a baseball game, the zoo, a faraway or nearby city, or an imaginary place. Pretend to ride the train to the destination and then talk about what you see, or get out and pantomime the action.

Transition Times

Moving from one activity to the next needs special consideration. A typical crisis in a classroom occurs when the whole class is ready to go outside except for one child who hasn't put the last touches on a craft or the last piece in a puzzle. Here are some ways of avoiding problems with transition times:

- Sing a special song or ring a bell five minutes before the end of an activity so that the children have time to get ready.
- Make clean-up time fun by having everyone join in singing a clean-up song.
- Sing a marching song or play "train" (children place their hands on the shoulders of the child in front) when you go to the playground or to a different room.
- Don't insist on perfection when children line up. They are not very good at it.
- Find fun ways of moving in a line, such as tiptoeing, walking with hands in the air, putting hands on heads, or singing a counting song.
- Plan for one of the staff in the room to move with the children when most of them are ready and for another staff to come and move with the stragglers when they are ready.

Scheduling and Planning for a Multiage Group

In scheduling the day for a family child care home or a multiage group at a center, you should begin by asking several questions:

- How many children are present?
- How many caregivers will care for the children?
- What are the ages of the children in care?
- What are the hours that the children will be in care?

Having infants and toddlers in care will mean creating a schedule where children eat, are diapered, and nap on their own individual schedules, with scheduled times for outdoor play or stroller rides.

Having preschoolers in care will require scheduling of large blocks of time for child-directed play. Meals/snacks, outdoor play, and naps/rest times will be scheduled at approximately the same times everyday.

The schedule for a homogeneous group in family child care will look very similar to a center-based child care schedule.

For a mixed-aged group, whether in center-based or family care, the provider will schedule those activities that need to get done in the day according to the needs of the children. Those activities will include the following:

- *Activities associated with the arrival of children*
- *Preparing and having meals and snacks.* Older children can help with setting the table and some simple food preparation. At the end of the meal/snack, the children can assist in the clean-up. Bottle-fed babies will have individual schedules for feedings.

- *Preparing for and naps/rest times.* Children take naps or rest depending on their individual needs. Babies may be awake during this time, if they recently have awakened from a nap.

- *Providing time for pretend play and child-directed play.* Most of the day should provide for child-selected and -directed play. This will allow you to change activities when children seem to be flagging and to bring babies in and out of the older children's activities, as appropriate.

- *Providing for music and creative arts.* As part of the self-directed play or in small groups, music and other creative arts activities need to be considered for all ages. Music activities and art/sensory activities especially lend themselves to mixed-age groups, so try to schedule them when the older infants and toddlers will be awake.

- *Providing for reading and literacy promotion.* Daily experiences with books and other literature need to be planned for all age groups. These should occur several times in the day, depending on the group in care and the length of time in care.

- *Providing for projects with wide age appeal.* Allow for thematic explorations that may extend over a period of time, such as putting on a play or rhythm band concert, visiting a zoo or farm and creating a mural or setting up a mini-zoo, celebrating a holiday, or planting a garden.

- *Observing children for program planning.* Plan a time when caregivers can look at individual children and record notes.

- *Preparing for children's departure.* Soon before the scheduled departure of the children, allow time for the caregiver to prepare the children and gather their belongings.

- *Keeping records and performing other administrative duties.* Time to maintain records and complete other required administrative duties also must be allowed. These tasks could typically be done when the children are napping, after the children leave, or at a set time, if there is more than one child care provider.

- *Diapering and using the bathroom.* Diapering and toileting are taken care of as needed.

- *Giving individual attention to children.* Children of all ages need individual attention. Be sure to schedule time for private conversations with each child. Also try to find time when you can follow the child's lead as you play together.

Other considerations for planning and scheduling should include the following:

- Balancing active and quiet activities
- Balancing whole-group activities—such as story reading, outings, cooking, some pretend play and art/sensory activities, music, and parachute play—with age-specific activities—such as sports, puzzles, games, and lessons
- Making schedules dependable but flexible
- Providing time for the caregiver to share ideas with parents

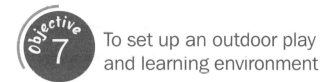

To set up an outdoor play and learning environment

The amount of time devoted to outdoor play will depend in part both on the ages of the children and the daily weather conditions. Regardless, every child care center should provide opportunities for children to spend part of each day outdoors.

"Musts" for the outdoor play area are as follow:*

- Forty-five square feet of space for every child over 2 years
- A 5-foot fence that completely encloses the play area and that has childproof latches on the exits
- Adequate shade
- Safe play equipment
- Adequate space between pieces of play equipment
- Soft surfaces under the climbing structures

Creating an Outdoor Play Area for Infants and Toddlers

Infants enjoy spending a part of the day outdoors. They can be placed in carriages, strollers, baby swings, or oversized playpens. Spreading a blanket on the ground also can allow for sensory play outdoors for infants. Crawling around on the blanket, feeling the warm breeze, watching the world around them, and watching soap bubbles are all enjoyable activities for infants.

Toddlers love the opportunity to play outside, as well. Outdoor play provides a chance to release energy, initiate games, and practice emerging motor and social skills with other youngsters. A toddler play area should include the following types of play opportunities.

Wheel Toy Section

Wheel toy play is particularly desirable for toddlers because it combines opportunities to practice motor skills with opportunities for pretending. A wheel toy area works best when it comprises a circular path that children can ride around. It also is an excellent idea to include a "service station," where wheel toys can be washed, oiled, fixed, and filled with gas.

> *Wheel toy play is particularly desirable for toddlers because it combines opportunities to practice motor skills with opportunities for pretending.*

Climbing Structures

Climbing structures for toddlers should take into account the fact that children this age may not be fully aware of their own capabilities and limitations. In selecting toddler structures, we cannot assume that the children's natural fear will keep them out

*Please check the regulations for your particular state.

of danger. A toddler who is learning to climb may climb to the top of a structure without concern for getting back down again. Make sure, therefore, that the height and construction of each structure minimizes the danger of a fall. Also make sure that climbing structures are placed on soft surfaces that comply with licensing regulations.

Many climbing structures have swing sets attached. In general, this is not a good idea. If a swing set is included in the toddler area, it should be a reasonable distance from other structures. Toddlers do not recognize the danger of running behind someone on a swing. Finally, the swings should be made of soft material.

Sandboxes and Sand Tables

Although 1- to 3-year-olds enjoy playing and digging in a sandbox or a sand table, doing so poses some problems that require special supervision:

- Toddlers are likely to throw sand at each other and take a bite of a sand "cake."
- It's difficult to convince toddlers to keep the sand inside the sandbox or sand table.
- Sandboxes can be breeding grounds for pinworms. (Sand tables are unlikely to present this problem.)
- Sandboxes and sand tables must be covered when not in use.

Despite these disadvantages, sandboxes and sand tables provide young children marvelous opportunities to fill and empty, to sieve, to pour, to experiment, and to pretend. If you have enough staff to maintain a sandbox, it deserves a place on the toddler playground.

Creating an Outdoor Play Area for Children 3 to 5

In designing playgrounds for children between 3 and 5 years old, consider the kinds of play that these children will engage in. The three kinds of play that children of this age enjoy are play for mastering motor skills, construction play, and representational play.

Play for Mastering Motor Skills

Because of the need for space and noise tolerance, the playground is the most logical place for large-muscle activity. As children run, climb, swing, and balance, they are learning to control their bodies, to understand spatial relationships, and to master a host of important motor skills.

Providing the following structures and equipment can foster motor skill development:

Structures

Jungle gyms	Tunnels	Basketball hoops
Slides	See-saws	Balance beams
Swings and tire swings	Log walks	

Equipment

Balls	Tricycles	Riding toys
Hoops	Wagons	Nerf bats and balls

Construction Play

A second type of outdoor play that children enjoy is *construction play*, where children experiment and create with different media. Construction play can take place with liquid, semiliquid, or solid materials. The following structures and materials can be used creatively in many construction play activities:

For Creating and Exploring with Liquid and Semiliquid Materials

Water tables	Sandboxes	Clay/soil digging areas

For Creating and Constructing with Solid Materials

Large, hollow blocks	Planks	Plastic crates
Cardboard cartons		

Representational Play

A third type of play that occurs on the playground is *representational play*, which parallels the imaginative play of the indoor environment. Children can vent frustrations, express feelings, and work out problems as well as engage in social interaction with their peers (perhaps even more so in this wide-open environment). Although children will use climbing structures and construction materials for imaginative play, their pretending can be enhanced by inclusion of some key props:

Climbing Area

Steering wheel on a "car"

Telephone

Row of tree stumps or plastic crates (for seats on a "train" or "bus")

Sandbox

Plastic animals and people	Shovels
Empty containers	Kitchen utensils, pots and pans
Cars, trucks, bulldozers, back-hoes, and boats (various sizes)	

Water Play

Empty containers	Baby dolls with soap
Objects that float/sink	

"Gasoline Station"

Clean, unused gas containers with spouts	Toy tools to repair cars
Money box with plastic coins to pay for gas	

Playhouse

Children love child-sized spaces. A well-equipped playground for young children should include a playhouse with a telephone and a shed that can be used for both imaginative play and storage. Because eating is so important to young children, pretend routines often revolve around playhouse activity. A picnic table with tableware is an excellent playhouse prop for encouraging pretending.

Science and Discovery

The outdoors is the perfect setting for science and discovery. Children have a natural curiosity about nature and living things. Taking nature walks and listening to nature sounds can add to the sensory experience of the outdoors. Simple and portable equipment that can enhance this experience includes the following:

Magnifying glasses	Bug catchers or plastic jars
Binoculars	Butterfly nets
Tools for digging and raking	

Also provide paper and writing instruments so that children can document their discoveries.

To ensure that the learning environment works for adults as well as for children

When asked what keeps them working in child care, most teachers and caregivers immediately say, "The children." Experienced professionals talk about the importance of their work. They enjoy watching young minds and personalities unfold and find that each day brings new discoveries and surprises. They know they are providing an important service to families and to society. Yet when pressed, these professionals often give another reason for staying in jobs that pay relatively low salaries: "I love the people I'm working with and the atmosphere of the workplace."

Child care centers and family child care homes can be special places for adults as well as for children. But this doesn't happen by itself. Conscious effort is needed to make spaces comfortable for child care workers and welcoming for parents.

Creating Spaces for Adults

Most child care centers have some spaces that are designed for adults: an office, a teachers' room and/or parents' room, adult-sized bathrooms, and a kitchen/work area that is off limits to the children. These spaces should be clean, bright, and cheerful, with comfortable furnishings, sufficient windows, attractive wall displays, plants, bulletin boards, and reading materials. An inviting place for adults to linger encourages communication. Having a few toys and children's books in these areas will help to welcome parents whose younger children are not in the center or who would like to spend some time with their child outside the classroom.

Although they are designed for children, classrooms also need to be set up with adults—teachers, parents, and classroom visitors—in mind. Each room should have these items:

- Comfortable seating for adults: a rocking chair in an infant or young toddler sleeping area, places to sit while feeding or eating with children, seating with back support for reading to children, and chairs that visitors can use
- A desk or other work and record-keeping station, conveniently located to allow simultaneous supervision of children who are playing or sleeping
- A secure place for the teacher's purse, briefcase, and other personal belongings
- Displays of children's work and words that let parents know what is happening in the classroom
- Pictures of the children's families and artifacts that represent their home cultures
- Pictures and artifacts that are meaningful to the teacher
- Inspirational posters, favorite quotes, and visionary messages that inspire adults who care for young children and reflect their wisdom
- Words in the children's home languages along with notes to parents in their home languages, when possible

- A bulletin board on which teachers and parents can post and exchange information
- A telephone

A learning environment for young children should be a place where their teachers, caregivers, and parents feel at home. The environment you create will be a reflection of who you are—your philosophy of teaching and learning, the things you love and want to share, and what you find beautiful, engaging, calming, and inspiring. It should be a place where you like spending time—a learning environment for adults as well as for children.

Additional Resources about Learning Environments

Bredekamp, S., & Copple, C. (Eds.). (1997). *Developmentally appropriate practice in early childhood programs* (Rev. ed.). Washington, DC: NAEYC.

Bronson, M. (1995). *The right stuff for children 0–8: Selecting play materials to support development.* Washington, DC: NAEYC.

Curtis, D., & Carter, M. (1996). *Reflecting children's lives: A handbook for planning child-centered curriculum.* St. Paul, MN: Redleaf Press.

Greenman, J. (1998). *Places for childhoods: Making quality happen in the real world.* Redmond, WA: Exchange Press.

Greenman, J. (1988). *Caring spaces, learning places: Children's environments that work.* Redmond, WA: Exchange Press.

Greenman, J., & Stonehouse, A. (1996). *Prime times: A handbook for excellence in infant and toddler programs.* St Paul, MN: Redleaf Press.

Harms, T., Clifford, R., & Cryer, D. (1998). *Early childhood environment rating scale–Revised.* New York: Teachers College Press.

Harms, T., Cryer, D., & Clifford, R. (2003). *Infant-toddler environment rating scale–Revised.* New York: Teachers College Press.

Hohman, M., & Weikart, D. (1995). *Educating young children.* Ypsilanti, MI: High/Scope Press.

Lally, R., Griffin, A., Fenichel, E., Segal, M., Szanton, E., & Weissbourd, B. (1995). *Caring for infants and toddlers in groups: Developmentally appropriate practice.* Washington, DC: Zero to Three.